BECOMING A CONSUMER PSYCHOLOGIST

W ritten by two scholars at the forefront of conducting research on the psychology of consumers and mentoring those new to the field, *Becoming a Consumer Psychologist* provides a guide to what it takes to become a consumer psychologist, and achieve success in this area.

Monga and Bagchi lay out the varied experiences that lead one to be a consumer psychologist in academia, marketing, or public policy. The book discusses the academic route in detail, guiding you on how to apply to schools, including for a Ph.D., what courses to take, and what to expect during your educational experience and after. It also discusses other routes that lead to diverse non-academic career paths in which practitioners apply their knowledge about consumer psychology.

The authors' guidance is backed by their own experiences as consumer psychology researchers, mentors, and journal Associate Editors; and the insights that the authors have gathered exclusively for this book from 23 other leading academics and practitioners. This book is essential reading for anyone looking to start their career in consumer psychology, and for mentors and advisors who are guiding students about career choices.

ASHWANI MONGA is Professor of Marketing at Rutgers Business School, and Provost and Executive Vice Chancellor at Rutgers University, Newark, USA.

RAJESH BAGCHI is Professor of Marketing and Department Head at Pamplin College of Business, Virginia Tech, USA.

BECOMING A CONSUMER PSYCHOLOGIST

Ashwani Monga and Rajesh Bagchi

Routledge
Taylor & Francis Group

NEW YORK AND LONDON

First published 2020
by Routledge
52 Vanderbilt Avenue, New York, NY 10017

and by Routledge
2 Park Square, Milton Park, Abingdon, Oxon, OX14 4RN

Routledge is an imprint of the Taylor & Francis Group, an informa business

Library of Congress Cataloging-in-Publication Data
Names: Monga, Ashwani, 1972– author. | Bagchi, Rajesh, 1975– author.
Title: Becoming a consumer psychologist / Ashwani Monga, Rajesh Bagchi.
Description: 1 Edition. | New York : Routledge, 2019. |
Includes bibliographical references and index.
Identifiers: LCCN 2019020401 (print) | LCCN 2019980759 (ebook) |
ISBN 9781138480858 (paperback) | ISBN 9781138480841 (hardback) |
ISBN 9781351061780 (ebook)
Subjects: LCSH: Consumers–Psychology. | Counseling.
Classification: LCC HF5415.32 .M6456 2019 (print) |
LCC HF5415.32 (ebook) | DDC 658.8/342023–dc23
LC record available at https://lccn.loc.gov/2019020401
LC ebook record available at https://lccn.loc.gov/2019980759

ISBN: 978-1-138-48084-1 (hbk)
ISBN: 978-1-138-48085-8 (pbk)
ISBN: 978-1-351-06178-0 (ebk)

Typeset in Minion Pro
by Newgen Publishing UK

For our parents who shaped our own psychology and our better halves who understand us better than we ourselves do; and for our teachers who helped us gain knowledge and our children who often test the limits of what we know.

CONTENTS

PREFACE

This book offers guidance to all who may want to become consumer psychologists. Whether one aims to conduct research in consumer psychology (e.g., at a university); or apply consumer psychology to reach out to consumers (e.g., via advertising) or to safeguard consumers (e.g., via public policy), we will provide a pathway to the reader—how to begin the journey, and what destinations to expect. In writing this book, we have relied extensively on our experiences as marketing professors. Our teaching and research relate to consumer psychology, we have mentored doctoral students who are now consumer psychologists themselves, we have published in the top journals in the area, we have served on the Editorial Boards of such journals (including as Associate Editors), and we have served in several administrative roles (including as heads of programs and departments). These experiences afford us a unique perspective that, we hope, the readers of this book will benefit from.

We do recognize our limitations. Although both of us have worked in the corporate sector, our experiences outside of academia are somewhat limited. Even within academia, our experiences are, well, just our own experiences. Therefore, to supplement our insights, we surveyed many others who work in consumer psychology within academia, as well as outside. We owe them a debt of gratitude: Wilson Bastos, Kerry Bianchi, David Brinberg, Kristina Durante, David Gal, Nitika Garg, Abhijit Guha, Paul Herr, Elise Ince, Matthew Isaac, Jesse Itzkowitz, Carl Marci, Steven Neumann, Priyali Rajagopal, Jose Ribas Fernandes, Ritesh Saini, Neela Saldanha, Gulen Sarial Abi, Julio Sevilla, Antonios Stamatogiannakis, Stephanie Tully, Dengfeng Yan, and Meng Zhu.

We would also like to thank the individuals who have shaped the experiences that led us to this book. The thoughts and ideas expressed herein are likely to cohere with those of our mentors, colleagues, and friends at the universities where we studied consumer psychology during our Ph.D.s (Ashwani: University of Minnesota; Rajesh: University of Colorado), and the universities that we have worked at (Ashwani: University of Texas at San Antonio, University of South Carolina, and Rutgers University; Rajesh: Virginia Tech).

Ashwani would not have taken even the first step toward his career in consumer psychology if it were not for his wife, Sonia Basu Monga. The two have been colleagues since they first joined SmithKline Beecham right after their MBAs. Thanks to a nudge from Sonia, both came over to the University of Minnesota for their Ph.D.s to begin their careers in consumer psychology. During the doctoral program, Ashwani benefited immensely from interactions with his advisor, Michael Houston, and mentors such as Akshay Rao. There were also several other faculty and students at the University of Minnesota who helped Ashwani advance his consumer-psychology career. Further mentorship and support came from individuals at the universities that Ashwani worked at: University of Texas at San Antonio, University of South Carolina, and Rutgers University. Particular thanks go to his four doctoral advisees who are now consumer psychologists in their own right: Robin Soster, Frank May, Rafay Siddiqui, and Ozum Zor. But Ashwani's key professional and personal support continues to be from Sonia, and now also from their wonderful daughter, Nirayka. Finally, this note of gratitude would be incomplete without the mention of the family that Ashwani grew up in: his parents and brother who always had more faith in him than he himself ever had.

Rajesh would like to extend his heartfelt gratitude to his faculty advisors and mentors. He would not have pursued a career in Consumer Psychology, had it not been for the astute guidance of his advisors, Dipankar Chakravarti and Atanu Sinha; and mentors, Amar Cheema and Paul Herr. Other people who have had a significant impact on his beliefs and thought processes include stalwarts in the field of consumer psychology, such as David Brinberg, Darren Dahl, Chuan He, Jeff Inman, Kent Nakamoto, and Akshay Rao. He would also like to thank all the faculty members of the Marketing Department at the University of Colorado at Boulder, without whose support and encouragement he could not have started his journey of being a consumer psychologist, and his student collaborators, Derick Davis, Stefan Hock, Daniel Villanova, Vivian Xie, and many others. He would also like to acknowledge his parents and sister, without whom he wouldn't be who he is; and his spouse, Amy, without whom he wouldn't be where he is. With a demanding day job and evenings also occupied with work related to consumer psychology, Rajesh wouldn't have the opportunity to pursue his passion, if it weren't for Amy's support. He would also like to acknowledge his children, Ryan and Tanya, who make him a better human being.

We would also like to thank Menatallah Walid, without whose help with research and collating materials, we would not have been able to finish this book. Our sincere thanks to the Routledge team, particularly Christina Chronister, for guiding us through the journey from proposing this book to writing it and seeing it in print. Finally, the two of us thank each other. As collaborators and friends, we have accomplished so much more together than we could ever have on our own.

Ashwani Monga and Rajesh Bagchi
July 8, 2019

ABOUT THE AUTHORS

Ashwani Monga is Professor of Marketing at Rutgers
Business School—Newark and New Brunswick, and Provost
and Executive Vice Chancellor at Rutgers University,
Newark. At the business school, he has previously served
as the Chair of the Marketing department, and as the Vice
Dean for Academic Programs and Innovations. He has been
conducting research in consumer psychology since his days
as a Ph.D. student in Marketing (with minors in Psychology
and Statistics) at the University of Minnesota, Twin Cities.
Ashwani is particularly focused on the psychology of time
and money (e.g., how consumers spend time differently
from money, and how time influences patience and
self-control). His research has been published in the most
influential journals of Marketing and consumer psychology.
He is an Associate Editor at the *Journal of Consumer
Research* and the *Journal of Consumer Psychology*; and is on
the Editorial Review Boards of the *Journal of Marketing*, the
Journal of Marketing Research, and the *International Journal
of Research in Marketing*. Ashwani's teaching, most of which
relates to consumer psychology, spans the undergraduate,

MBA, Ph.D., and Executive Education programs. In the premier consumer-psychology organization, the Society for Consumer Psychology (Division 23 of the American Psychological Association), he has served as the Education and Training Chair, advising students interested in pursuing careers in consumer psychology, and organizing dissertation proposal competitions. He has also been the coordinator of a doctoral program in Marketing, and the dissertation chair for several doctoral students conducting research in consumer psychology. For the inaugural MSI Scholar Awards of 2018, the Marketing Science Institute included Ashwani among 34 faculty members worldwide who were recognized for excellence in Marketing scholarship. In addition, he has received several teaching awards, and has been honored with outstanding reviewer awards from the *Journal of Consumer Research* and the *Journal of Consumer Psychology*. Ashwani is privileged to share a home with the joys of his life: his wonderful wife Sonia, and terrific daughter Nirayka.

Rajesh Bagchi is Professor of Marketing and Department Head at the Pamplin College of Business, Virginia Tech. After completing his undergraduate degree in Civil Engineering, Rajesh pursued a master's degree in Environmental Engineering. After that, he worked in several high technology startups and then, after a few years, decided to pursue his doctoral degree in Marketing from the University of Colorado, Boulder. In his research on consumer psychology, Rajesh studies the psychological processes that underlie consumer and managerial decision making. His research is primarily focused on two areas: (a) how numerical markers influence consumer judgments and behaviors, and (b) how consumers form pricing judgments. Rajesh often draws from and contributes to several literatures, such as those on numerical cognition, numerosity, goals, consumer financial decision making, and pricing. His research has been published in several journals such as the *Journal of Consumer Research,* the *Journal of Marketing,* the *Journal of Marketing Research,* the *Journal of Public Policy and Marketing,* the *Journal or Retailing*, and *Marketing Letters*. Rajesh serves as an Associate Editor for the *Journal of Consumer Research* and is on the Editorial Review Boards of several other journals. He was ranked among the Top 30 most productive scholars worldwide based on publications in Marketing's premier journals over a ten-year period (2009–2018). He was also selected as a Young Scholar by the Marketing Science Institute in 2013 and received an Early Career Award from the Society for Consumer Psychology in 2016. Rajesh teaches Marketing Analytics and Marketing Research at the undergraduate level, and Judgment and Decision Making at the doctoral level. Rajesh is married to Amy Pruden-Bagchi, and they have two adorable children, Ryan and Tanya.

CHAPTER ONE

The Field of Consumer Psychology

The American Psychological Association (APA) recognizes consumer psychology as a sub-field that deals with theoretical psychological approaches to understanding consumers (APA Division 23: Society for Consumer Psychology). This sub-field has traditionally been seen as an offshoot of social psychology. According to *Encyclopedia Britannica*, whereas social psychology is the "scientific study of the behavior of individuals in their social and cultural setting," consumer psychology is a "branch of social psychology concerned with the market behavior of consumers."

The field of consumer psychology has broadened over the years, with insights from social psychology blending with those from other areas of psychology (e.g., cognitive psychology, which is concerned with learning, behavior, and other aspects of human cognition). Insights have also come in from related fields such as economics. In particular, behavioral economics research by Nobel Laureates Daniel Kahneman and Richard Thaler (and their collaborators such as Amos Tversky) has nudged consumer psychology toward understanding the heuristics and biases that underlie consumers' judgments and decisions. These different perspectives have turned consumer psychology into an interdisciplinary area encompassing diverse topics such as consumers' memory, learning, preferences, biases, customs, and so on. An understanding of such topics is of interest to academic researchers trying to get a better grasp on consumers and marketplaces. It is also at the heart of all business enterprises targeting consumers, and others that support such enterprises, including marketing research firms and advertising agencies. Such an understanding is also critical for public-policy makers trying to promote consumer welfare and prevent predatory business practices.

WHO IS A CONSUMER PSYCHOLOGIST?

Given the diversity in professions that consumer psychology interfaces with, it is often hard to describe who exactly a consumer psychologist is. After all, "consumer psychologist" is not usually a job title that is written on the business cards of individuals. Rather, this phrase characterizes the type of work that comprises different professions.

We, the authors, consider ourselves consumer psychologists because of the kind of research that we conduct. Ashwani tries to understand the psychology of time and money. For instance, he has shown that consumers use short-cuts in information processing (i.e., heuristics) much more when decisions relate to spending time rather than spending money. Think of the time that consumers spend on searching, such as in going from one store to another to find the perfect pair of shoes. What Ashwani and his co-author have found is that consumers do not systematically treat time expenditures the way they treat money expenditures (Monga and Saini 2009; Saini and Monga 2008). Rather, they simply use a heuristic such as "visit three stores" while giving little consideration to how much time it takes to visit each store.

Rajesh tries to understand consumers from multiple perspectives, but particularly with respect to how consumers approach the goals that they have, and how they process numerical information. For instance, he has shown that loyalty programs are viewed differently depending on whether the program is structured using small numbers (earn 1 point per dollar and redeem $6 when you have 100 points) or large numbers (e.g., earn 10 points per dollar, and redeem $6 when you have 1,000 points). Note that the two formats are mathematically identical but result in different preferences under different conditions because of how consumers process numerical information (Bagchi and Li 2011).

Regardless of the specific research questions that are pursued, the eventual goal of consumer psychology is to understand consumers' thoughts, feelings, and actions as they interact with products, services, and ideas in the marketplace (Peter and Olson 2017; Hoyer and MacInnis 2007; Schiffman and Kanuk 2000). Thus, consumer psychology is focused on a "consumer" interacting in a "marketplace." A "consumer" chooses how to spend resources in return for market-related benefits. The resources could be varied, such as money, effort, and time spent deliberating about a purchase. The benefits could also be varied, such as acquiring a product or gathering information about where to shop. The "marketplace" often refers to online and traditional retail establishments such as grocery stores. But consumers interact not just with stores, but also with other marketplaces in which they make choices, such as those relating to health (e.g., which doctor to visit) and finances (e.g., which brokerage firm to use). The personal goals of consumers also intersect with the marketplace. For instance, consumers' weight-loss goals influence what they buy at the grocery store. Their self-imposed restraints on shopping for clothes have implications for the apparel industry. And their targets for retirement savings hold consequences for financial services firms.

Consumer psychologists examine the "who," "what," "when," "where," and "why" of decision making (Hoyer and MacInnis 2007; Schiffman and Kanuk 2000). Who is making the decision—is it one individual or a group (e.g., a restaurant choice by an individual vs. a family), and who is the decision for: oneself or someone else (e.g., a health decision for oneself vs. one's child). What is the decision—is it to make a purchase or is it to defer the purchase and gather more information? When is the decision being made—early on in a planned manner or in a rushed manner at the very last minute? Where is the decision made—at home or inside a store? Why is the decision made—to simply take care of a problem or for some aspirational goal? In fact, the "why" is perhaps the most important aspect explored by consumer psychologists. If one is able to understand the "why"—the factors and processes underlying consumers' decisions—one can better predict what may happen in different consumption situations.

DIVERSE PROFILES OF CONSUMER PSYCHOLOGISTS

The reasons for figuring out the psychology of consumers are varied. A consumer psychologist at a university may be trying to advance a general understanding of consumers; a marketer may be trying to influence consumers in a certain way; and a public-policy maker may be trying to improve consumer welfare. In the previous section, we offered the reader a glimpse of the kind of research that we conduct. However, our intention is not to limit this book to our own perspectives. Rather, we wish to share insights from consumer psychologists across a wide spectrum of industries and backgrounds in order to give a sense of what this field encompasses. With that objective in mind, we reached out to several leading experts.

Some of these individuals were known to us through personal and professional interactions, and others were selected based on their public profiles (e.g., on LinkedIn). We then emailed all a survey with several questions related to their careers. Many of them (23 in all) very graciously agreed to share their insights with us. While all 23 individuals saw themselves as consumer psychologists in a broad sense, this does not mean that their work is exclusively about consumer psychology. Consider one individual who completed our survey, David Brinberg. Although he has contributed extensively to consumer psychology, and is a leading expert, he has also contributed to other areas and commented accordingly: "I think my interests align with research areas in consumer psychology, but not exclusively in that domain." It is safe to assume that most others who completed our survey are also not working exclusively in consumer psychology. But their work does connect closely to consumer psychology and they are recognized leaders. Because of this, we incorporated their excellent insights while writing this book. We remain forever indebted to them and we believe readers will benefit tremendously from their input. They are listed below in last-name-alphabetical order, with a mention of their educational and professional profiles (at the time they responded to our survey).

1   Wilson Bastos
    Position: Assistant Professor of Marketing, Catolica
        Lisbon School of Business and Economics, Portugal
    Degrees: Bachelor of Science, International Business
        Administration; Master of Business Administration,
        Marketing; Doctor of Philosophy, Marketing

2   Kerry Bianchi
    Position: Chief Executive Officer, Visto
    Degrees: Bachelor of Arts, Psychology

3   David Brinberg
    Position: R.O. Goodykoontz Professor, Virginia Tech
    Degrees: Bachelor of Science, Psychology; Master
        of Science, Psychology; Doctor of Philosophy,
        Psychology

4   Kristina Durante
    Position: Associate Professor of Marketing, Rutgers
        Business School

Degrees: Bachelor of Science, Mass Communication; Master of Arts, Social Science; Doctor of Philosophy, Psychology

5　David Gal

Position: Professor of Marketing, University of Illinois at Chicago

Degrees: Bachelor of Science, Computer Science; Master of Science, Management Science and Engineering; Doctor of Philosophy, Business Administration

6　Nitika Garg

Position: Associate Professor, University of New South Wales

Degrees: Bachelor of Science; Master of Business Administration; Doctor of Philosophy, Marketing

7　Abhijit Guha

Position: Assistant Professor, University of South Carolina

Degrees: Bachelor of Arts, Economics; Post Graduate Diploma in Business Management; Master of Business Administration; Doctor of Philosophy, Marketing

8　Paul Herr

Position: Virginia Carolinas Professor of Purchasing Management, Virginia Tech

Degrees: Bachelor of Arts, Psychology; Doctor of Philosophy, Social Psychology

9   Elise Ince
    Position: Associate Professor of Marketing, University
        of South Carolina
    Degrees: Bachelor of Science, Business and Economics,
        Accounting; Master of Management, Marketing;
        Doctor of Philosophy, Marketing

10 Mathew Isaac
    Position: Associate Professor of Marketing, Seattle
        University
    Degrees: Bachelor of Arts, Biology; Master of Business
        Administration, Finance/Strategic Management;
        Doctor of Philosophy, Marketing

11 Jesse Itzkowitz
    Position: Senior Vice President and Behavioral
        Scientist, Ipsos Behavioral Science Center
    Degrees: Bachelor of Science, Psychology; Doctor
        of Philosophy, Cognitive Psychology; Doctor of
        Philosophy, Marketing

12 Carl Marci
    Position: Executive Vice President/Chief
        Neuroscientist, Consumer Neuroscience, Nielsen
    Degrees: Bachelor of Arts, Psychology; Master of Arts,
        Psychology; Doctor of Medicine

13 Steve Neumann
    Position: Principal, Cardinal Points Consulting
    Degrees: Bachelor of Arts, English; Master of Arts,
        Advertising

14 Priyali Rajagopal

Position: Associate Professor, University of
North Texas

Degrees: Bachelor of Commerce, Accounting; Post
Graduate Diploma in Business Management,
Marketing; Doctor of Philosophy, Marketing

15 Jose Ribas Fernandes

Position: Associate, BEworks

Degrees: Doctor of Medicine; Doctor of Philosophy,
Neuroscience

16 Ritesh Saini

Position: Associate Professor, University of Texas at
Arlington

Degrees: Bachelor of Engineering, Mechanical
Engineering; Master of Business Administration;
Doctor of Philosophy, Marketing

17 Neela Saldanha

Position: Director, Centre for Social and Behaviour
Change, Ashoka University, India

Degrees: Bachelor of Arts, Economics; Master of
Business Administration, Marketing; Doctor of
Philosophy, Marketing

18 Gulen Sarial Abi

Position: Assistant Professor of Marketing, Bocconi
University, Italy

Degrees: Bachelor of Arts, Business Administration;
Master of Science, Management Research; Doctor of
Philosophy, Business Administration

19 Julio Sevilla
    Position: Assistant Professor, University of Georgia
    Degrees: Bachelor of Science, Industrial Engineering;
        Master of Business Administration, International
        Business; Doctor of Philosophy, Marketing

20 Antonios Stamatogiannakis
    Position: Assistant Professor of Marketing, IE Business
        School, IE University
    Degrees: Bachelor of Science, Business Administration;
        Master of Science, Marketing; Doctor of Philosophy,
        Consumer Behavior

21 Stephanie Tully
    Position: Assistant Professor, Stanford University
    Degrees: Bachelor of Science, Business Administration/
        Marketing; Masters of Philosophy, Marketing;
        Doctor of Philosophy, Marketing

22 Dengfeng Yan
    Position: Associate Professor, New York University
        Shanghai
    Degrees: Bachelor of Science, Political Science; Master
        of Philosophy, Marketing; Doctor of Philosophy,
        Marketing

23 Meng Zhu
    Position: Associate Professor, Johns Hopkins
        University
    Degrees: Bachelor of Arts, Literature; Master of Science,
        Industrial Administration; Doctor of Philosophy,
        Marketing (minor: social decision sciences)

As should be clear from the above, consumer psychology underlies a varied set of job profiles. The predominant job profile matches that of the authors of this book— marketing professors who conduct research on consumer psychology and teach courses related to it. Examples of academics from the list above include David Gal, a Professor at the University of Illinois at Chicago, and Stephanie Tully, an Assistant Professor at Stanford University. Within international schools, Dengfeng Yan is an Associate Professor in China at the Shanghai campus of New York University, and Wilson Bastos is an Assistant Professor in Portugal at the Catolica Lisbon School of Business and Economics. While the research areas of these faculty vary greatly, it is important to note that consumer psychologists within academia share many similarities such as participating in similar conferences (Association for Consumer Research, Society for Consumer Psychology, etc.) and publishing in similar journals (*Journal of Consumer Research*, *Journal of Consumer Psychology*, etc.). It is outside of academia that the heterogeneity in roles is more evident. To take a few examples from the list above, Kerry Bianchi is Chief Executive Officer at Visto, an Enterprise Advertising Hub that optimizes advertising expenditures for several firms; Jessse Itzkowitz is Senior Vice President and Behavioral Scientist at Ipsos, one of the world's leading market research agencies; and Steve Neumann spent his career in consumer insights at several consumer healthcare companies, and is currently a Principal at Cardinal Points, a consulting firm focused on health and wellness. Thus, in diverse areas such as advertising, market research, healthcare companies, and consulting firms, individuals with varied titles are engaged in work that relates to consumer psychology. We will revisit the profiles of these individuals, and others, in the next few chapters as we explore what it takes to become a successful consumer psychologist.

CHAPTER TWO

Studying to Become a Consumer Psychologist

Consumer psychologists who work within academia invariably have a doctoral degree in marketing or related fields such as psychology. But consumer psychologists who work outside of academia don't have a uniform academic background.

DIVERSITY IN EDUCATIONAL PATHWAYS

There is a lot of diversity in the educational pathways of the consumer psychologists on our panel. Kerry Bianchi has a Bachelor's degree in Psychology; Steve Neumann has a Bachelor's degree in English and a Master's degree in Advertising; Jesse Itzkowitz has a doctoral degree in Marketing; and Carl Marci, in addition to having Bachelor's and Master's degrees in Psychology, also has a Doctor of Medicine degree. Despite disparate educational pathways, all these individuals have excelled in their consumer-psychology careers.

Although having an educational background in psychology is not necessary—many learn through experience—it is not a coincidence that many consumer psychologists have studied in psychology departments or in marketing departments where the psychology perspective is dominant. There are also several other departments that may provide psychological insights, including communication, advertising, human ecology, home economics, consumer, apparel, and retail studies, hospitality and tourism, and so on. Indeed, consumers are at the heart of many disciplines because the reactions of consumers determine the success of initiatives in many different arenas. For example, while the field of public policy may be interested in instituting policy to nudge consumers to improve their welfare, policies that are implemented without taking consumer reactions into account are unlikely to succeed. Thus, while it is not critical that one's major in college be psychology, it is certainly helpful if one's major provides a psychological perspective that may lead to a career in consumer psychology. An undergraduate degree may sometimes suffice, as is clear from the terrific careers of those we surveyed. However, we recommend that students give serious consideration to a graduate degree—a doctoral degree if one is aiming for a consumer-psychology career in academia, and at least a Master's degree if one is targeting a career outside of academia.

GRADUATE DEGREES IN CONSUMER PSYCHOLOGY

Master's programs give students more intense exposure to both substantive and methodological aspects relating to consumer psychology. Such Master's programs usually cater to two groups of students: those who wish to be applied consumer psychologists, and those who wish to segue into doctoral programs. A Master's program in marketing or psychology is perhaps most relevant although, as noted earlier, consumer relevant research is also conducted in other disciplines. Master's programs range from one-year versions to two-year versions, and usually offer more flexibility in curriculum than undergraduate programs. For example, New York University's Master's program in Psychology allows students to specialize in Social and Consumer Psychology. Students are required to take a couple of substantive introductory courses in Consumer Behavior and Social Behavior, followed by a set of electives, which range from the psychology of decision making to the psychology of social media. Courses on gender roles, diversity, and culture and society, allow students to appreciate the impact of larger contextual factors in influencing consumer psychology. Students also take courses in research methodology, including advanced courses in statistics. Some other Master's programs, such as those offered at Seoul National University and Rotterdam School of Management, also cover journal articles pertaining to consumer psychology, making such programs more research based and similar to doctoral programs. In fact, many Master's programs also offer an option to write a Master's thesis, which could be a synthesis of knowledge in the field, but may also entail original work conducted by the student under the guidance of an experienced faculty member. Such a thesis allows students to put the knowledge assimilated from course work to a real test of creating knowledge, uncovering deeper insights into consumer psychology.

While a Master's degree may be sufficient to be an applied consumer psychologist, a doctoral degree is usually required for a career in academia. In a Ph.D., students dig much deeper into how consumers process information and how different factors influence consumers' decisions. Students also master the tools required to uncover insights that have not yet been discovered. As part of their dissertation, students may advance a completely new theory on, say, how consumers make decisions in risky situations, discover a new heuristic that comes into play, or identify the conditions that determine differences in information processing. The goal of a doctoral program is to create scholars who are not only knowledgeable enough for pedagogical purposes, but are also expanding the knowledge base of consumer psychology.

COURSEWORK RELATED TO CONSUMER PSYCHOLOGY

At the undergraduate level, psychology majors may take intensive psychology courses, but they are unlikely to specialize in understanding the consumer perspective. Marketing majors, in contrast, may not have the extensive breadth of psychology majors, but are more likely to be exposed to the theories and methodologies used to understand consumer decision making and behavior. For instance, an introductory course on Consumer Behavior may provide substantive knowledge about topics such as how consumers process information, how they make decisions, and how they respond. Some topic areas covered may include attitude theory, persuasion, advertising strategy, branding, social influences on consumer behavior, consumer biases, cross-cultural differences, ethics and public policy, and so on.

Although courses such as Consumer Behavior provide an overview of the area of consumer psychology, undergraduate students in Marketing usually don't have the opportunity to take more in-depth courses. Such courses are often available at the graduate level in Marketing, Psychology, and other areas. For example, students may take a deep dive into the topic of memory and learning to understand how consumers process and encode information. Likewise, students may take advanced courses on how consumer attitudes are formed, and the consequences for decision making. Another major area of relevance is the study of heuristics and biases. While traditional economists may assume that consumers are rational and make unbiased decisions after carefully considering all the relevant information, this assumption may not always hold. When buying products, for instance, do we always compare all the prices and buy the best product at the best price? Sometimes we may work hard to do so—for example, when making an expensive purchase—but we may not do so when buying regular grocery items. This is because research suggests that consumers are cognitive misers, and do not always have the ability, willingness, and opportunity to process information deeply. They often use shortcuts, which are referred to as heuristics. For example, consumers may assume that a larger package—say, a package of 38 diapers—will give them better value (i.e., lower per-unit cost) than a smaller package of

19 diapers. This heuristic of inferring value from package size may indeed work at times, but may lead to biased decision making on other occasions.

Courses at the graduate level also provide a better sense of how seemingly independent topics of studies are intricately connected. After all, consumer decisions are not made in a vacuum but in the context of many intervening factors. For instance, decision making may be influenced by consumers' own motivations and also the social context in which those decisions are made. Thus, an individual who is motivated to lose weight may eat smaller portions, particularly when being observed by others, consuming just enough that may be considered socially desirable. But the same individual may have no inhibitions eating large portions in the company of close friends. In fact, because eating with friends is an enjoyable activity, spending more time eating may extend the enjoyment. To understand such nuanced aspects of consumer psychology, it is usually necessary to take more in-depth courses that capture the latest findings in scholarly journals. Thus, to understand the nuances of how consumers process price information, one could take specialized courses in pricing that draw upon not only traditional topics such as perception, information processing, and motivation, but also rely upon recent research advances in areas such as numerical cognition, which capture how individuals process and encode numerical information. As just one example, we often encounter prices with ".99" endings, such as a shirt priced at "$9.99" as opposed to "$10." It is because research suggests that consumers may interpret $9.99 as $9 plus some change. In contrast, a price of $10 may be coded in memory as $10, resulting in the perception that a $9.99 price is much lower than $10, a judgment that is not warranted by a 1 cent difference in price. Such conclusions are often drawn from carefully designed experiments that control for extraneous influences. Participants are randomly assigned to the experimental conditions of a manipulated independent variable to examine how it causes changes in a dependent variable. Thus, price presentation could be manipulated to examine how it causes changes in the willingness to purchase the product.

Just as a student may get insights into substantive issues such as pricing, other courses may offer insights into advertising, retail management, and so on. These insights into different facets of consumption are usually provided by courses offered by Marketing departments. For an ideal mix, such courses need to be complemented by courses offered by Psychology departments, which provide depth into the fundamental aspects of the human mind.

In addition to understanding the substantive issues related to consumer decision making, it is also important to understand the methodologies used to study this area. For example, to make the inference that a $9.99 price is judged as being lower than a $10 price, consumer psychologists need to master different methodological approaches and procedures. Thus, courses in marketing research, experimental methods, and analytics may be relevant. A course in marketing research, for example, may provide an overview of the different methodological approaches that can be used to study consumer psychology. Some consumer psychologists analyze data using statistical tools—such as regressions and correlations—while others use more qualitative approaches to understand patterns. Although secondary data is also used at times (e.g., sales data of firms), consumer psychologists primarily rely on an experimental paradigm. Therefore, they need to have a deep understanding of the experimental method, as well as nuances involved in questionnaire design. That may entail understanding how each question is written, how these questions relate to the hypotheses, and how to test these hypotheses using appropriate methodology. Thus, an introductory course in Marketing Research may cover the market research process, research design, design of questionnaires, and other topics including qualitative and observational approaches. These would be supplemented with appropriate methodologies, such as correlation analysis, regression, and analysis of variance.

At the graduate level, students often need to take advanced courses to handle complex research questions. Consider a question of how advertisements that are run in November may affect sales. The effect of advertising in November may generate sales not just in November, but also in December and January. Moreover, other intervening factors could also impact sales, such as holiday shopping, and the contemporaneous actions of competitors during the holiday season. Additional environmental factors, such as how well the economy is doing, are also likely to impact consumer behavior. To do justice to collecting and analyzing data in these multifaceted situations, graduate courses often offer more specialized courses that undergraduate programs do not. While we highlight the importance of graduate courses, we should reiterate that, at least for non-academic positions, relevant work experience may compensate for the lack of a graduate degree. And for those who do pursue graduate degrees, undergraduate students with psychology or marketing majors may have an advantage, but they are not the only ones pursuing graduate degrees in areas related to consumer psychology. Students come from varied backgrounds, including the arts, literature, and the fields of STEM (Science, Technology, Engineering, and Math).

CHAPTER THREE

What Consumer Psychologists Do

As mentioned earlier, "consumer psychologist" is not a specific job title that individuals have, but refers to the type of work that a diverse group of professionals are engaged in. Thus, a professor may conduct research on consumer behavior, an advertising professional may try to understand how to get a message across to consumers, a marketing researcher may try to figure out consumers' reactions to a new product, or a researcher at a government agency may try to understand how to protect consumers from being swindled. All of these jobs are different, but what binds them is a common goal to understand the processes that guide the thoughts, feelings, and behaviors of consumers as they interact with products, services, and ideas in the marketplace. But, of course, there are unique aspects to these roles as well.

To provide a few examples of what consumer psychologists do, let us start with a rather famous sports event that occurs in February—you guessed it, the Super Bowl! While teams clash on the field, do you know where the real competition is? On television. Companies compete against each other, paying as much as $5 million for a 30-second advertisement, vying for the attention of millions of Americans. How do you think these advertisements were developed? Consumer psychology is at the very center as firms think carefully about the message that they want to convey about themselves and their products, and how they want to execute that message. Even within the same category, brands vary in how they reach their audience. Taking the example of insurance brands, Geico may use humor to reach consumers whereas Allstate may use emotional appeals. To make such choices, companies and advertisers rely on the methods of consumer psychology. For instance, utilizing theories on how different messages may be processed under different levels of involvement, advertisers may frame the right message. Additionally, they may employ experimental methods to test which of different advertisements has the intended impact, whether that be on brand recall, purchase intention or any other metric. An advertising agency may test the advertisements with a small sample of customers before going for a national launch. This testing becomes especially critical for Super Bowl advertisements, which are viewed by millions of people, and cost millions of dollars to run. Therefore, advertisers pay careful attention to first understanding the psychology of their customer base, and then designing the best messages to persuade them.

An understanding of consumers is helpful not just for creating messages, but also for figuring out the right outlets from which to sell one's products. Imagine that you are the manager of Prada, a high-end manufacturer of luxury products. Where would you sell your women's handbags? Would you consider Walmart? After all, think about the number of stores Walmart has, and how almost all of us visit Walmart at some point (ok, maybe not the uber rich— but you get the point). Consumer psychologists step in to assess decisions such as these, and will perhaps conclude that Prada's brand image is inconsistent with the image of Walmart. Given that people shop at Walmart to "save money," a rather expensive luxury brand is unlikely to be the right fit. Thus, Prada may not want to be associated with Walmart. For that matter, being associated with expensive Prada products may also damage Walmart's "save money" positioning. To understand such effects, one needs a keen understanding of the tools and methods of consumer psychology to identify which brands may or may not fit with each other (e.g., Prada may not fit with Walmart but may be a good fit for Nordstrom), and which product category may make sense for a particular brand, and which category may not (Prada milk, anyone?).

Consumer psychology plays a critical role in public policy contexts as well. For example, if the Consumer Financial Protection Bureau needs to mandate the disclosure of certain information by firms, they first need to rely on an understanding of consumer psychology to see how the disclosure information may be interpreted—how the right amount of information may improve consumer welfare, but how information overload could possibly be unhelpful. Those involved with public policy can employ consumer psychology to enhance the welfare of consumers in many ways, including protecting them from predatory practices, helping them save more money for retirement, and enabling them to lead healthier and more fulfilling lives. In short, consumer psychologists can help businesses who are trying to reach customers while also helping public-policy makers who are trying to protect customers from overreach.

CONSUMER PSYCHOLOGISTS AT UNIVERSITIES

D espite the consumer-psychologist roles described above, it needs to be noted that the most common role for a consumer psychologist is as a university professor. While consumer psychologists work most often in Marketing or Psychology departments, work related to consumer psychology is conducted in other departments too. For example, the University of Wisconsin-Madison's School of Human Ecology has faculty studying consumer behavior and home economics. Likewise, at Purdue University, the department of Consumer Science is housed under the auspices of the College of Health and Human Sciences. Other examples include the University of Chicago's Behavioral Science Department and University of North Carolina's Consumer, Apparel and Retail Studies department, among others. In terms of teaching, consumer-psychology faculty members are more likely to gravitate toward courses such as Consumer Behavior, Judgment and Decision Making, and Marketing Research. In terms of research, the area of consumer psychology is very broad and ever expanding; so it is difficult to objectively assert the boundaries. But in general, the focus of consumer psychology is to understand the psychological processes that underlie consumer judgment and decision making and its associated antecedents and consequences. Depending on their expertise and interest, professors may use behavioral, sociological, and quantitative approaches in understanding consumer behavior and its implications. To develop their insights, behavioral researchers draw from research in psychology, marketing, economics, and even neuroscience. It is important to note that academic consumer psychologists are focused on theoretical psychological phenomena, and not on specific direct applications, such as how a grocery store can sell more bread. However, as they say, there is nothing more practical than a good theory. Therefore, theories related to consumption often have wide applications in Marketing, public policy, and other areas. An analogy that is commonly used to describe this perspective is the fisherman versus the marine biologist. The fisherman may be interested in catching fish, but the marine biologist is interested in understanding fish. Similarly, the consumer psychologist attempts to understand consumers.

To provide a sense of the kind of consumer-psychology research that is conducted in academia, let us provide a few examples of our own work. Imagine that you just bought a book online. Rather, disappointingly, the bookstore informs you that the book delivery will be delayed by a week. That is a bummer. Now, what if instead of a week, this delay was expressed as a seven-day delay? In Monga and Bagchi (2012), we rely on research on numerical cognition to show how consumers are influenced by the units of time—a seven-day delay may seem longer than a one-week delay, but the reverse can happen in some cases. How we express numbers also affects other decisions. Imagine iTunes running a special promotion of "$29 for 70 songs." Bagchi and Davis (2012) show that this deal seems worse than a deal of "70 songs for $29." That is, even with identical information, the piece of information that comes first (the benefit of songs vs. the cost in dollars) is weighted more, leading to different perceptions of the same deal. As yet another example, Siddiqui, May, and Monga (2017) examine the time window of consumption, which is the duration within which a product needs to be consumed (e.g., an expiration period). They find that time windows may help consumers achieve their self-control goals of consuming virtue products at a higher rate and vice products at a lower rate. With product quantity constant, the results show that a short window (i.e., high rate of consumption) nudges individuals toward virtues whereas a long window (i.e., low rate of consumption) nudges them toward vices. Thus, time windows are not passive constraints for consumers but active determinants of their product preference; such windows can serve as a tool for consumers' self-control.

While the above hopefully gives you some sense of what consumer psychologists like us do, let us now provide a broader sense by referring to our panel of consumer psychologists. Specifically, we asked them why they saw themselves as consumer psychologists—what they did, and which elements of their jobs related to being a consumer psychologist. The answers we received are varied, and we report them in verbatim (Appendix A). But let us highlight a few themes that arise from their responses.

The academics in the panel are focused on their research and teaching. On the question of how he saw himself as a consumer psychologist, Ritesh Saini succinctly replies "as a researcher and teacher" and Abhijit Guha mentions "I teach consumer behavior…and I research consumer behavior…" This sentiment is common across the faculty members in our panel because their research is in consumer psychology, and they often teach courses that relate to consumer psychology (consumer behavior, marketing research, etc.). However, what is interesting is that even though all academics in our panel are in marketing departments, their specific consumer-psychology identity is quite salient to them. Wilson Bastos explains how the marketing community does not adequately convey the benefits of marketing to society and expresses pride in being a researcher who studies the consumer, rather than marketing in general. Moreover, what is studied is often determined by the questions that evoke one's curiosity. As Elise Ince notes about taking inspiration from her lived experiences, "I also continuously question and analyze my environment, as well as my interactions with others, to look for interesting effects to study." The dominant methodology used by these academics is experiments, in which researchers determine the causality of an independent variable (e.g., motivation) by setting up different experimental conditions of the variable (e.g., low vs. high motivation) and then assessing the impact on the dependent variable of interest (e.g., whether one attends to the core message of an advertisement or to peripheral aspects that are not central to the message). Regarding the reliance on experiments, Kristina Durante explains "I also consider myself a consumer psychologist because I experimentally manipulate the environments in which people are making consumer decisions in order to measure how these manipulated factors can change purchase decisions." But, regardless of the method used, the defining characteristic of consumer psychology is a focus on consumers. In the words of David Gal, "I've become less tied to methodology and more focused on using any method." Thus, while the experimental method is dominant, many consumer psychologists are willing to rely on any quantitative or qualitative method that helps them derive deeper insights into consumer psychology.

Regarding substantive topics, while a focus on consumers is common, the questions explored are quite different. The topics studied include judgment and decision making (Mathew Isaac, Julio Sevilla, Meng Zhu), consumer reactions to the marketing mix (Dengfeng Yan), responses to psychological threats (Gulen Sarial Abi), information processing and memory (Priyali Rajagopal), the antecedents of consumption (Paul Herr), consumer motivations and emotions (Nitika Garg), social issues and group behavior (David Brinberg), and material versus experiential purchases (Wilson Bastos). Thus, even in our small group of academics, there is a lot of diversity with regards to the kinds of consumer psychology topics that they study.

CONSUMER PSYCHOLOGISTS OUTSIDE OF ACADEMIA

This diversity in what individuals do as consumer psychologists is even more evident outside of academia.

With a focus on advertising effectiveness, Kerry Bianchi, Chief Executive Officer at Visto, talks about how her consumer-psychology work relates to eliciting a response from the consumer, ranging from brand awareness to eventual engagement. Jesse Itzkowitz, Executive Vice President and Behavioral Scientist at Ipsos, discusses how most of his time is spent on using behavioral science to "help identify and influence the nonconscious factors that drive consumer goals, consumer beliefs, and ultimately—consumer decisions." Jose Ribas Fernades, Associate at the consulting firm BE-Works also applies behavioral science as a practitioner, using a mental framework of consumer psychology. Behavioral science can also be used in the social sector, as is done by Neela Saldanha, Director of the Center for Social and Behaviour Change, who states that "All marketing problems are fundamentally consumer psychology problems." For Carl Marci, Executive Vice President and Chief Neuroscientist at Nielsen, his work as a consumer psychologist involves using neuroscience and other physiological measures to get insights into consumers' emotional responses. Steve Neumann, who has spent most of his career in consumer healthcare and is currently a consultant, views consumer psychology from a broad perspective as "understanding why people do the things they do when exploring and making purchase choices for goods and services and what they think and how they behave afterwards." This perspective may characterize all practitioners of consumer psychology, though the specific activities that they are engaged in are quite diverse.

We would encourage the reader to look at the verbatim responses (Appendix A) to get a more complete sense of how our panel of academics and non-academics thinks of consumer psychology, and the elements of their job that relate to being a consumer psychologist.

CHAPTER FOUR

Graduate Studies in Consumer Psychology

As described earlier, the journey to becoming a consumer psychologist often involves going through graduate school. In this section, we will provide details on a typical graduate program in marketing that consumer psychologists usually go through. However, note that many of the same factors may play a role in graduate degrees in related disciplines (e.g., psychology).

CHOOSING GRADUATE SCHOOLS TO APPLY TO

Most consumer psychologists have a Ph.D. in Marketing because interest in consumers and consumption is most intense within Marketing departments in business schools. However, several consumer psychologists also come from the field of psychology and other areas. These different journeys are reflected in our panel of academics. While most in our panel have Ph.D.s in Marketing (Wilson Bastos, David Gal, Nitika Garg, Abhijit Guha, Elise Ince, Mathew Isaac, Priyali Rajagopal, Ritesh Saini, Gulen Sarial Abi, Julio Sevilla, Antonios Stamatogiannakis, Stephanie Tully, Dengfeng Yan, and Meng Zhu), several do have Ph.D.s in psychology (David Brinberg, Kristina Durante, Paul Herr). In the discussion below, we will focus more on a typical program of a consumer psychologist in academia, which is a Ph.D. in Marketing, though many of the same ideas would also apply to other Ph.D. programs.

Given the high commitment needed to earn a Ph.D.—usually 4–6 years—it is critical that one chooses the right graduate school. In a typical five year program, students usually take courses during the first two years and focus much more on research during the remaining three years. If the goal is to obtain a faculty position in research-oriented institutions, then it would be important to pay attention to the research credentials: school and department ranking, faculty expertise, culture of the place, and job placement.

Ranking. Several ranking lists are available to assess a university's productivity in the top journals of the field. These include the University of Texas at Dallas rankings (UTD) and the Financial Times list (FT), among others. We suggest that you give consideration to both current ranks as well as ranking information over the last five years to get a sense of the sustained performance of a school. The journals most likely to be outlets for consumer psychology research, and which are listed in the UT Dallas ranking are the *Journal of Consumer Research*, *Journal of Marketing*, and *Journal of Marketing Research*. These three journals, along with the *Journal of Consumer Psychology*, also appear in the FT ranking. These rankings are important because they provide a sense of the research productivity of the department and, consequently, the probability that a doctoral student will be able to publish in these journals. Making progress toward such journal publications is critical to obtaining jobs at top-tier research institutions.

Faculty expertise. Go through the websites of different departments to see what topics the faculty are interested in, and if they have been publishing consistently in their areas of interest. Research active faculty members provide guidance and advise what is needed to publish in the top journals. Most important, a graduate student's interests need to cohere with the expertise of the faculty. It is not enough to have highly accomplished faculty members, if they conduct research in areas that a student is not really interested in. Also, see if the department faculty offer a sufficient breadth in interests. Keep in mind that your own interests may change through the program; so having breadth in the department makes it more likely that you will find a match. Also, such breadth can offer a more well-rounded education, and prepare you better for the long run.

Culture and Facilities. Both departmental and school culture are important to your well-being during the program. For instance, effective departments usually have an open-door policy where doctoral students are free to stop by the offices of whomsoever they wish, and choose research advisors that they prefer. Other schools may require that you work only with specific assigned faculty, which is perfectly fine as long as you are sure about whom you want to work with. Regarding research culture, it is also important to see if students are given the opportunity to get started on research early, rather than being told to hold off until all coursework is completed. Given the competitive marketplace, a culture of getting started early may be beneficial to your success. Also, it is important to assess what kinds of facilities exist to aid in research (e.g., behavioral lab that can be used for experiments, and research budget to support conference travel). We should note that the culture may vary widely across disciplines. For instance, if Ph.D. students in a psychology department are recruited based on a faculty member's funding status, then the student may be recruited for that specific faculty member and not have the option to choose another advisor. Of course, no model is perfect. What is important is the right fit between what an applicant is looking for, and the culture and facilities available in a specific department.

Job Placements. A well-ranked research school that has appropriate faculty expertise and a supportive culture and facilities should yield a good placement of its doctoral students. Schools should be able to provide such data for the last 5–10 years. Such data presents the "base rate" of what your placement is likely to be. Of course, the final outcome would be based on your own performance, but the base rate should give you a broad sense of how you may be placed if you join that school. It may also be useful to pay attention to the very best placements over the years as an indication of what a motivated student can possibly achieve.

GETTING INTO A GRADUATE SCHOOL OF CHOICE

Once you have chosen the schools that you are most interested in, the next step is to have a strong application so that you can get in. The application deadline is usually in January or February, with programs beginning in the Fall (usually August/September). To apply, students are required to submit a curriculum vitae, a statement of purpose, transcripts, letters of recommendations, and test scores: Graduate Management Admission Test (GMAT) or the Graduate Record Exam (GRE), along with evidence of English proficiency for international applicants, such as the Test of English as a Foreign Language (TOEFL). Some programs may ask for additional information as well.

Usually a graduate program committee evaluates the applicant pool and makes recommendations to the Department Head or the Ph.D. Director of the school. Because most (but not all) Ph.D. programs in Marketing provide funding to their admitted students, there is high selectivity, with only a couple of students admitted per year (though some departments may accept more students—the University of Wisconsin-Madison's Consumer Behavior and Home Economics doctoral program sometimes admits several students in the same year). Decisions are made quickly and on a rolling basis, with students receiving offers in February/March, needing to confirm their decisions by April.

As mentioned above, students in Marketing departments are often fully funded—tuition is covered and an additional stipend is paid. In return, students are usually required to work on research with faculty and provide research/teaching assistance for up to 20 hours a week. This is not always the case in other disciplines—some guarantee funding, while others offer some form of funding, albeit competitively. Psychology departments sometimes offer students research grants and research fellowships that result from faculty grants (from Government and Federal institutions, such as the National Science Foundation, National Institutes of Health, and even private institutions). In the case of such funded grants, faculty hire graduate students to help with their research.

The best Ph.D. candidates are secured via an extensive process. The graduate program committee usually makes decisions based on the following materials provided by the applicant:

Curriculum Vita. This should provide a summary of all your achievements including your educational background, detailing your major/minor course of study along with graduation dates. This document should also contain information about your extra-curricular activities, work experience, as well as any other information that you feel may be relevant.

Statement of Purpose. This document should discuss why you are interested in the specific program, how your background qualifies you for this position, what kind of research you would like to do, and what you would like to do with your degree. Therefore, it is important to study the department carefully and orient your statement to be consistent with the strengths of the department and faculty in the department. The graduate committee pays very careful attention to this document as it helps them understand how important the particular program is to you, and how determined you are. This is because Graduate school can be challenging and requires determination, focus, and enthusiasm.

Educational Background. The committee looks at the transcripts to assess the educational background of the applicant. While a stellar record is not necessary, it undoubtedly helps. Many successful students have had a solid educational background, comprising a roster of high-level courses with good grades. But keep in mind that many students also express their abilities and motivation in other ways, such as their work on interesting projects with faculty members.

Test scores. The committee also pays careful attention to the students' test scores, such as the GMAT and GRE. A high score can do wonders for your application. For international students, tests assessing proficiency in English, such as the TOEFL, is also required.

Letters of Recommendation. These letters are critical to understanding not just how qualified you are to enroll into graduate school but also what kind of a person you are. Are you diligent? Do you work hard? Do you take initiative? Are you a critical thinker? Do you have a pleasant demeanor? Do you work well in groups? Can you work independently? Your letters should indicate some of these elements, such as your qualifications, your commitment, and your potential to do well. The committee may also reach out to the letter writers for further clarification.

DOING WELL IN
GRADUATE SCHOOL

A s we noted earlier, graduate programs usually vary in length from 4–6 years, while five years is the norm. Thus, a sustained work ethic is necessary to do well in a Ph.D. program. During the course of the program, students are expected to take several courses, including coursework in content and theory, statistics, research methodology. Usually, students are also encouraged to take a minor. The minor is usually consistent with the student's interests and professional goals. Commonly selected minors include psychology, economics, sociology, management, management science, and statistics.

A series of doctoral courses is often required during the first year of study. Several of these courses focus on the substantive literature and current issues in academic research in the field. Students are also expected to complete several courses on research methods. In addition, at least some graduate-level statistics courses must be taken beyond introductory statistics courses. Students are also expected to take a few courses in their chosen minor field, as stipulated by the school. We strongly urge that you choose courses that are of interest to you, so that you are motivated to go deeper and perform well.

As the student advances through the doctoral program, the focus of the program shifts from coursework to research activity. At the end of the first or second year, students may be required to take a qualifying examination that builds on the work completed to date. This requirement varies from school to school. Some schools require that students pass an exam set over several hours while others require students to submit an original research paper. This step is very critical because students who fail the qualifying examination are usually asked to leave the doctoral program.

During the second or third year, students may be expected to create a dissertation committee. The dissertation committee usually consists of the student's primary advisor, and a few other committee members (often between three and five). The committee is created in consultation with the dissertation chair. Students usually develop their dissertation proposal during the third year, which they then defend in their third or fourth years. Subsequent years in the doctoral program are focused on pursuit and completion of dissertation research. The final oral examination, including the defense of the dissertation, is administered after completion of the written dissertation. As the dissertation phase is rather unstructured, it is very important that a student remains in constant contact with the dissertation advisor in order to make sure that milestones are crossed at appropriate intervals.

In addition to coursework and research, teaching is a key commitment at many doctoral programs as well. We discuss all three aspects in detail below.

Coursework. You may be required to take between 9 and 12 credits of coursework each semester during the first two years in the program. Usually these courses are chosen in consultation with the Graduate Program Director. You may be required to take courses that are offered by the Department's faculty. It may be a good idea to also take other relevant courses outside of your home department. Depending on your interests, you may consider courses in areas such as psychology, economics, sociology, statistics, and education. It may be a good idea to take as many methods courses as possible, so that you are at the cutting edge of the methodologies employed in the research that interests you.

Graduate courses are different from typical undergraduate courses. These courses require a lot more preparation and engagement. While some of the courses are lecture-based (particularly the methods courses), many of the other courses tend to be discussion-based. To provide enough time for discussion, graduate classes usually meet once a week for a longer duration (rather than twice a week for shorter durations). Students take a wide variety of courses that help them gain substantive knowledge about the area as well as learn about the methodologies used to understand consumer decision making and behavior. Students may take courses such as Consumer Behavior, which discuss issues relating to how consumers process and interpret information. Additionally, they may take a course such as Judgment and Decision Making, which is grounded in behavioral decision research, and provides a framework for understanding the normative and descriptive principles that govern consumer judgments and decisions. Topic areas covered may include an overview of the field, heuristics and biases, mental accounting, framing and context effects, and other areas. In addition to understanding the substantive issues relating to consumer decision making, it is also important to understand the methodologies used to study consumer psychology. Such courses may include experimental design, regression analysis, and so on.

While the methodology courses may involve textbooks, the substantive courses such as Consumer Behavior and Judgment and Decision Making usually entail reading papers from the top journals in the field. These might include articles published in top marketing journals, such as the *Journal of Consumer Research*, *Journal of Consumer Psychology*, *Journal of Marketing*, and the *Journal of Marketing research*, as well as articles published in top psychology journals, such as the *Journal of Personality and Social Psychology* and *Psychological Science*. The articles may also come from business journals that are outside of Marketing but frequently publish research relevant to the field of consumer psychology, such as, *Organizational Behavior and Human Decision Processes* and, of course, more broad-based scientific outlets such as *Science*.

For such doctoral courses, faculty usually assign several discussion articles for each lecture. The faculty member may take the lead on some courses, whereas students are expected to take the lead on some others. The selected papers include both foundational seminal work as well as more contemporaneous literature from the top journals. The papers are typically discussed in class in detail—students are not only expected to learn the material covered but use this opportunity to critique these papers and think about ways to expand on these findings. After these discussions, the instructor might provide an overview and draw on other relevant work in the area. The manner in which students are evaluated in such classes is also different from similar courses taught in the undergraduate program. Here is an example of evaluation criteria as well as course expectations from the syllabus of a doctoral course, Consumer and Managerial Judgment and Decision Making, which is taught by one of the co-authors of this book (Rajesh).

Evaluation criteria	Contribution
Presentation of assigned research papers	25%
Discussion of research papers (presented by other students)	25%
Idea write-up and discussion	10%
Proposal (due at the beginning of class on November 18)	40%

Leading discussions of assigned papers: All students are expected to read all the papers. However, students will be assigned specific papers to lead discussions on. Students should plan to spend approximately 30–35 minutes leading the discussion of the paper. The student leading the discussion should prepare a 1–2 page handout to circulate in class.

Contributing to discussions: All students are expected to read, print out, and bring in all the readings for each class. All are expected to contribute to the discussions in class. Instead of quantity, the focus will be on the quality of your comments.

Idea write-up: Starting week 3, the instructor will include one "mystery article" in each class. This article will not be "directly" related to the other focal articles. The students' task, however, will be to come up with a research idea that combines ideas presented in the core research articles with this mystery article. They will need to write a one-page brief discussing their idea along with one or two hypotheses and an explanation of why they expect this. They will need to present this idea to all the students in class.

Research paper proposal: Students are expected to submit a research paper proposal outlining a decision making problem of interest to them (no longer than 10 double-spaced pages, 12-point font, 1-inch margins). This proposal should apply some of the relevant concepts discussed in the seminar and should propose how you would study the phenomenon (using experiments, empirical analysis of secondary data, or analytically). They will also need to present this proposal to the class.

Research. An integral component of doctoral programs is to develop doctoral candidates who are capable of conducting high-quality research. In order to be successful in this, you must learn how to think independently as well as understand the nuances of the research process. As discussed earlier, it is important to be at a supportive school where you have the support to conduct good research, and start on research projects early on in the doctoral program.

While focusing in an area is good, particularly in the early stages of your career, also keep in mind that eclecticism is also great. The key thing is to pick topic(s) that you really enjoy working on. The rewards of publications are few and far in between—it is imperative that you enjoy the overall process of conducting research.

Teaching. Although the expectations of teaching vary from one school to the next, most schools usually expect students to teach courses in their third or fourth years. Teaching assignments are usually made by the Department Head in consultation with the Graduate Program Director. Because teaching is an important component in a faculty member's life, it is important that you learn pedagogical skills by availing of the opportunities available within your school.

What we described above were the steps involved in getting into graduate school and being successful there. However, the journey of becoming a consumer psychologist does not always need to involve graduate school and, even when it does, the journey may be triggered by happenstance, as it did for many of our panelists. It is important to be open to such opportunities and take advantage of them to further your career.

To get a sense of the journey that others have gone through, we asked our panelists how they ended up becoming consumer psychologists. The reasons were varied, such as informal conversations with more advanced doctoral students (Wilson Bastos), doing a senior thesis during the undergraduate program that provided clarity on one's interests (Kerry Bianchi), striking a fortuitous collaboration with someone at the Food and Drug Administration (David Brinberg), taking some psychology courses while working (Kristina Durante), having roommates that happened to be enrolled in Ph.D. programs (David Gal), enjoying Marketing as a subject (Nitika Garg), enrolling in a program that sparked interest (Abhijit Guha)), mere curiosity (Paul Herr), a process of eliminating topics that one does not like (Elise Ince), conducting interviews as part of one's job (Mathew Isaac), a desire for change (Jesse Itzkowitz), being approached by a business student (Carl Marci), getting a first-hand view of human behavior (Steve Neumann), the nature of one's job (Priyali Rajagopal), a yearning to solve applied problems (Jose Ribas Fernandes), interest in psychology as a teenager (Ritesh Saini), enjoying a summer training (Neela Saldanha), meeting with a professor who evoked interest (Gulen Sarial Abi), enjoying a particular course (Julio Sevilla), being an intuitive psychologist from a young age (Antonios Stamatogiannakis), reading pop books (Stephanie Tully), being fascinated by firms' branding strategies (Dengfeng Yan), and pure randomness (Meng Zhu). The verbatim responses (Appendix B) provide more insight into how these individuals stepped onto the journey that eventually led them to consumer psychology.

As should be clear from the above, there is not a single path toward the consumer psychology journey. In our opinion, nothing substitutes for personal interactions with those working in consumer psychology. A good step would be to look up the faculty profiles of universities, and then individually contact one or two professors whose work may interest you. Set up a meeting and ask them what their work life is like—what they find fulfilling and what frustrates them. It may be fruitful to read some of their work before you meet them so that you can signal that you are seriously considering this profession, and also have something tangible to have your conversation around. Talking with a few consumer psychologists would help you get a better sense of whether this path is really for you and, if so, how you can become a consumer psychologist yourself.

CHAPTER FIVE

The Destination of Consumer Psychologists

As discussed earlier, consumer psychologists can be found in many domains, but most are in academia. Therefore, we will first cover the academic life in detail— applying for faculty positions and then doing well in those positions. We will then briefly discuss some other destinations as well.

APPLYING FOR A FACULTY POSITION

In many ways, the process of applying for faculty positions is similar to that of applying for graduate school. Prior to applying, you need to research schools carefully. Schools vary in terms of their focus. Some position themselves as research institutions, others position themselves as teaching institutions or as balanced institutions. Research schools will typically give a lot more importance to research, though this does not mean that they expect sub-par teaching. It just means that they have higher research expectations and better facilities to conduct research. They may have lower teaching loads to compensate for higher research expectations but you would still need to be a good and dedicated teacher. In contrast, teaching schools typically will have lower research expectations and may not have the same level of support to conduct research. Teaching loads may also be higher and you may be expected to excel at teaching. Balanced schools tend to prioritize both research and teaching, though the expectations for both will be somewhat more reasonable. For a successful academic career, finding the right balance between one's strengths and the focus of a school is important. To get a sense of which doctoral students joined which schools over the past several years, a good resource is the "Who Went Where" report issued by the American Marketing Association's Doctoral Student Special Interest Group (Docsig.org).

Many of the aspects that go into selecting an appropriate university to join as a faculty member are the same ones that are used when selecting a university to join as a doctoral student. In particular, four aspects are the same as those discussed in Chapter 4: ranking, faculty expertise, culture and facilities, and job placements of doctoral students. This last point is important because a strong doctoral program suggests a strong research culture that may enhance faculty productivity. Of course, there are some strong Marketing departments that may not have a doctoral program but, in general, a vibrant doctoral program helps maintain a vibrant research culture. Both the authors have worked in institutions with doctoral programs and have found working with doctoral students very rewarding; they bring in research energy and interesting perspectives that also help faculty grow as researchers. Finally, another point to note when considering a school for a faculty position is the path to tenure. Expectations vary from one school to the next, and clarity is needed on this front.

SECURING A JOB AS A FACULTY MEMBER

Once you have chosen the schools that you are most interested in, the next step is to apply. In the paragraphs below, we will focus on securing a job as a tenure-track faculty member. However, we should inform the reader that there is a growing trend to hire professional-practice faculty members who are recruited primarily for their teaching (given their extensive experience in the corporate world). Because these faculty members are usually less focused on research, the following discussion is not oriented toward them. Rather, it is oriented toward faculty positions that do involve research as a major component: tenure-track positions in which the starting position is that of an assistant professor.

If you are applying for positions in Marketing departments (as most consumer psychologists do), you would prepare to go on the market a year before you graduate. You would prepare materials such as a curriculum vitae, a cover letter, copy of published or working papers, and letters from your recommenders.

Curriculum Vita. This should provide a summary of all your achievements including your educational background that details your major/minor course of study along with graduation dates. This document should also contain information about your research and teaching. Provide a short discussion of your research interests. List all your publications (if you have any) and your current research projects (including your dissertation). Some applicants include brief abstracts of their projects in the appendix. We suggest that you include information about any courses that you have taught and the teaching evaluations. Also include any service accomplishments and awards that you may have received.

Cover Letter. This document should discuss your teaching and research interests, why you are interested in the specific position, how your background qualifies you for that position, and what kind of research you would like to do going forward. The search committee pays very careful attention to this document as it helps them understand how coherent your research and teaching interests are and how well you will fit in their department. Keep in mind that while it is good to have specific research interests, you do not want to position your interests so narrowly that it limits the departments that may perceive you to be a good fit with the faculty members.

Research Record. The research record matters, particularly so for research schools. It is not very common for students to have published papers when applying for faculty positions, but most students will have some research papers that are currently in the review process—either just submitted or in an advanced round (i.e., have been invited to revise the manuscript based on reviewer comments). Depending on the type of school (research, teaching, or balanced), this component of your vita will be evaluated very carefully. The best research schools would want to see publications in the top journals, or at least papers in the review process (those in advanced rounds of review will be weighed much more than those just submitted). This is perhaps the most important piece of information research schools pay attention too. Balanced schools will also pay attention to your research record. While they may not expect you to have published papers in top-tier journals, having papers in advanced rounds will be very helpful and may give you an advantage. To some extent, even teaching schools would want to see a promising research portfolio. Note that while the journal is a signal of the quality of a research article, recruitment committee members often read candidates' articles themselves to assess the merits of the work. Committee members especially rely on their own opinions when external validation is not yet available (e.g., the manuscript has not yet received a revision opportunity from a reputable journal).

Letters of Recommendation. These letters are critical to understanding not just how qualified you are to secure a faculty position but also what kind of a person you are. Usually one letter is written by the chair of your dissertation committee, while the other two (or more) letters are written by faculty members who are committee members or who you have research collaborations with. The focus of these letters is on your research and teaching credentials. The letter also highlights faculty's observations about your personality. The committee may also reach out to the letter writers for further clarification. Note that the recommendation from the dissertation advisor is usually weighted very heavily in hiring decisions.

With all the materials in hand, you would apply to universities around the end of June. Faculty search committees usually meet in early July to discuss applications (though some schools may have earlier deadlines). The shortlisted candidates will then be contacted for initial interviews that may sometimes be held remotely (e.g., over Skype), but are most often held at the Summer Educator's Conference of the American Marketing Association (AMA). The AMA conference is typically held in the month of August although the exact dates and location vary. The AMA interviews last for anywhere between 30–60 minutes. Afterward, schools shortlist the candidates they are most interested in—usually between three and five for each position—and invite them to campus for a more extensive interviewing process. At the conclusion of all the candidate visits, sometime around November, schools make decisions about who should be offered the job. Once you receive an offer, you may be given a couple of weeks to accept it. If you reject it, the offer may then go to the next candidate in the list. We should highlight that this process applies more to schools within the U.S. and less to many other schools across the world. While some do follow the U.S. timeline, many others may have their own timelines that one should attend to (if interested in such schools). Even within U.S. schools, the AMA conference is not the be all and end all of recruiting. Many schools also recruit outside of the regular summer cycle, finding great candidates in what is informally known as the "winter market."

DOING WELL AS A FACULTY MEMBER

Most faculty are initially hired at the assistant professor level. This is a probationary role during which candidates are assessed based on research, teaching and, to a lesser extent, their service (e.g., on school committees). After a certain period of time, they are evaluated and are then either promoted to the position of associate professor with tenure, or asked to leave the university (i.e., tenure is an up-or-out decision). While the timeline for this promotion varies from one university to another, a six-year tenure clock is most common. Note that anonymous letters from external reviewers at other institutions (usually experts in your area of research) play a major role in tenure and promotion decisions—these letters serve as external validation of your performance.

Although all institutions judge faculty based on their research, teaching, and service, the weight of each of these varies as a function of the institution. As noted earlier, some intuitions focus more on research, others on teaching, while several others espouse a balanced approach. Research institutions will likely pay more attention to your research—the number and quality of your publications— when making tenure decisions. Teaching institutions may pay more attention to your teaching—the number of classes taught and your overall performance as assessed by student evaluations, peer reviews, and other means. Balanced schools will pay moderate attention to both. Although service also plays an important role, the expectations for untenured assistant professors are usually quite limited, with the expectations being much higher for those at the associate and full professor ranks. Here are some more details on each of these three components: research, teaching, and service.

Research. One way to be productive is to have research projects that are connected to each other at some broad level. We believe that conducting programmatic research has many benefits. You understand an area well because of which you also understand the gaps in the literature well. You not only develop strong conceptual skills but also learn how to test your ideas effectively in that particular domain. The field also recognizes you as an expert in the area, which has other perks. For example, you may be asked to review the research of other scholars or even be invited to join the editorial review boards of journals.

Teaching. You may be expected to teach anywhere from three to eight courses per year, depending on your institution. Teaching assignments are usually made by the department head in consultation with you. Because teaching is an important component in a faculty member's life, it is important that you learn the pedagogical skills necessary to be an effective teacher. We suggest that you make your teaching as efficient and effective as possible. Put in a lot of work initially to build your slides and teaching materials and then update them periodically whenever you teach.

Service. To be a good, valued, citizen of the school, it is important to contribute on committees both within the department and in the school as a whole. Most universities function using a model of shared governance, where all stakeholders (students, faculty, and others affiliated with the university) share the burden, and work together to ensure that the university functions efficiently. While service activities take time, it is certainly time well spent because such activities give faculty, especially new hires, a chance to connect with other faculty members and staff whom they may not usually meet. You will also get a deeper understanding of the culture of your department and university and will have an opportunity to shape policies and procedures that have important implications for all stakeholders.

NON-ACADEMIC DESTINATIONS

As we mentioned earlier, academia is not the only destination of consumer psychologists. While the world of academia is fairly straightforward for consumer psychologists with a defined path of entering a Ph.D., conducting research, and joining an academic institution, the paths outside of academia are much more varied. The individuals we profiled for this book have had very successful careers, but they did not follow one particular route. Rather, they studied different kind of topics and worked in diverse areas before they stepped into a role that involved a heavy reliance on consumer psychology. Thus, it is impossible to provide one specific road map for the non-academic route as we did for the academic route.

The individuals whom we profiled for this book are in diverse areas such as advertising, market research, healthcare companies, and consulting firms. Their titles vary, but their work is squarely focused on consumer psychology. Examples include Kerry Bianchi, who is Chief Executive Officer at Visto, an Enterprise Advertising Hub that optimizes advertising expenditures for several firms; Jessse Itzkowitz, who is Senior Vice President and Behavioral Scientist at Ipsos, one of the world's leading market research agencies; and Steve Neumann, who spent his career in consumer insights at several consumer healthcare companies, and is currently a Principal at Cardinal Points, a consulting firm focused on health and wellness. As should be evident from these disparate careers, consumer psychology is a way of understanding the world, with this understanding being at the core of many professional areas.

CHAPTER SIX

Continuing on the Consumer Psychology Journey

Given that you are reading this book, it is clear that you have already started on your journey toward becoming a consumer psychologist. As you continue your exploration, keep in mind that this is a long journey that would require a serious commitment for an extended period of time. While we are excited to get more people interested in consumer psychology—indeed, that is why we wrote this book— we also want to make sure that you get a sense of what consumer psychologists truly like and dislike about their chosen profession, so that you have a balanced view of what lies ahead in this profession.

POSITIVES AND NEGATIVES OF THE JOURNEY

For those in academia or outside, the destination of being a consumer psychologist is usually one that individuals are happy with. For us, the authors, this continues to be a very fulfilling journey and we wanted to write this book as a way to share our thoughts with others and take them along on this amazing ride. However, as is clear from the verbatim responses of our panel (Appendix C), while there are indeed several things to like about being consumer psychologists, there are some things to dislike as well. So let us give you a quick overview of the likes and dislikes that we gathered from our panel.

A fundamental aspect that academics appreciate is the freedom to work on interesting research projects of their choosing. As Wilson Bastos notes "Being able to understand why and when...people do what they do is simply amazing!" According to Julio Sevilla, "I like the flexibility and freedom of deciding what topics and research questions I want to study and to be able to decide how I want to approach it." Many also commented on how this profession of conducting research on consumer psychology involves a perpetual creation of new ideas. In the words of Kristina Durante, "Creating knowledge is truly entrepreneurial..." Moreover, the possibility of studying topics that are inherently interesting excites academics and non-academics alike. As Kerry Bianchi notes, "I think the study of human behavior is endlessly fascinating." "I enjoy thinking about problems," mentions David Gal. The different steps that go into conducting research excite researchers such as Stephanie Tully, who mentions "I love theory creation, designing studies, and analyzing data."

For consumer psychologists, figuring out the "why" of a consumer phenomenon is particularly gratifying, as it is at the core of an innate human quest to understand the world. Neela Saldanha enjoys thinking about "why people might want to do something and especially all the counter-intuitive reasons that they may not." For Antonios Stamatogiannakis, "The best thing is that I can mentally challenge myself about understanding virtually any behavior that I see in my everyday life." Understanding the "why" is also critical for those outside of academia. Jesse Itzkowitz argues how behavioral science helps give businesses the "why, which they can then use to replicate success in analogous situations." After all, unless one understands why something works and why it does not, it would not be possible to deliver consistent success. Sharing an understanding of consumer psychology with others is also a source of joy to many, such as Julio Sevilla, who mentions that "I also enjoy sharing my knowledge with students and the opportunity to play an important role in their professional and personal foundation."

A common theme regarding what academic consumer psychologists dislike is the grueling journal review process that can take a toll on the best of researchers (though academics do appreciate the valuable role that the review process plays in the entire scholarly enterprise of evaluating each other's work). As Priyali Rajagopal notes, "It took me a while to realize that research and publication are two different processes that require very different skill sets." In the words of Stephanie Tully, "The only part I do not love is the review process." Another issue that many researchers find challenging is a consistent drive toward "interesting" findings. As noted by Antonios Stamatogiannakis, "The tough part is to find explanations that are considered 'interesting' by today's standards." For some consumer psychologists, particularly those working in the social sector in developing economies, it can also be frustrating to see a research community that is skewed in a different direction. As Neela Saldanha mentions, "most consumer psychologists are in US universities and cater to richer populations. Understanding the consumption choices of the poor would be wonderful." Even in the industry, some dislike the slow adoption by consumer psychologists of newer techniques, such as those from neuroscience. Carl Marci notes "I dislike the rapid changes and lack of sophistication of many people in the industry. Traditional marketing training lacks a neuroscience perspective."

Thus, as should be clear from the above, being a consumer psychologist is a mixed bag. So, you, the reader, need to figure out whether the path is a net positive for you, as it is for the consumer psychologists that you read about in the book. We, the authors, agree that not everything is perfect in the world of consumer psychology. At the same time, the challenge of figuring out the psychology behind the consumption phenomena that we see around us in the world, and conducting studies to pin down the "why" of consumer-relevant phenomena is extremely gratifying and more than makes up for the challenges. We are both very excited that we got into this field and would very gladly do this all over again. If you are on board with us, then read on to get some words of advice from the consumer psychologists in our panel.

WORDS OF ADVICE FROM A FEW CONSUMER PSYCHOLOGISTS

The verbatim words of advice are noted in Appendix D. Some advice pertains to developing your own self. For instance, Wilson Bastos asks you to "Accept the reality that you are often wrong in your thinking, and seek the truth." Steve Neumann believes that it is critical to have "an insatiable curiosity about why people are making the choices they do." Some other advice pertains to affiliating with like-minded and motivated people in the field. Paul Herr suggests that you "Pick your colleagues carefully" and Meng Zhu asks that you "find a core group of similarly minded friends," David Brinberg wants you to "be open to the ideas of smart people, find colleagues you like, enjoy and who you can find laughter with, and spend time simply exploring ideas and problems."

In Appendix D, you will also find plenty of additional useful advice from our panel of consumer psychologists, which we hope you pay heed to. To summarize the key points, you are advised to read broadly and deeply (Wilson Bastos), to be open to non-linear career paths (Kerry Bianchi), to be around smart colleagues (David Brinberg), to focus on Ph.D. programs that relate to Marketing (Kristina Durante), to be wary of the competition (David Gal), to have passion for what you study (Nitika Garg), to go in with some practical experience (Abhijit Guha), to pick your colleagues carefully (Paul Herr), to start on research early (Elise Ince), to study psychology (Matthew Isaac), to be fluent in the literature of consumer behavior (Jesse Itzkowitz), to get a solid education in psychology (Carl Marci), to develop a solid foundation (Steve Neumann), to develop excellent written and oral communication skills (Priyali Rajagopal), to have a passion for academic rigor (Jose Ribas Fernandes), to have a widespread theoretical education (Ritesh Saini), to explore different paths (Neela Saldanha), to stay connected with other researchers (Gulen Sarial Abi), to take your time to be informed (Julio Sevilla), to be methodologically rigorous (Antonios Stamatogiannakis), to enjoy the process of research (Stephanie Tully), to focus on ads as much as the shows (Dengfeng Yan), and to be persistent (Meng Zhu).

We completely agree with all of the above comments and suggestions. What we would like to further reinforce is that as students, it is important to learn as much as you can—to develop a strong and deep understanding of the area. Whether for substantive or methodological courses, do not hesitate to take the most challenging ones that expand your horizons. To be successful in the long run, it is important to be genuinely passionate about your chosen research area, and to be intellectually curious. It is also important to be intellectually humble—after all consumer psychologists dedicate their lives to understanding others, and so it is important to remind oneself that there is always more to learn. In this process of learning new things, your core beliefs about how consumers think, feel, and act may change. Be open to this. We also believe that it is important to choose your collaborators carefully. It is perhaps even more important to choose your mentors carefully. They will play a very critical role in not just shaping your thought process but also influencing your career and life more broadly. The two of us have been very fortunate in that we have had great mentors, colleagues, and collaborators. We hope that you benefit from such good fortune as well.

Finally, please pay attention to Appendix E, where we have the responses on the question of how the field of consumer psychology is evolving, and what lies ahead. One key trend here is the greater influx of technology and the availability of big data. Kerry Bianchi notes how "Extracting data will need to keep pace with the new ways we can deliver experiences to consumers." Looking at the future of consumer psychology, Dengfeng Yan also mentions how "I guess it's already more technology- and data-driven and will be even more so in the future."

Another trend that is dominant, and particularly relevant for those in academia, is that the number of top journals has not kept pace with the quality of research being produced by an increasing number of consumer psychologists. Consequently, the path to publishing is becoming more challenging year after year. According to David Gal, "My perception is that the field is getting more competitive and that the demand for publications is correspondingly increasing." This competitiveness has become even more challenging as researchers are required to meet a high bar for transparency and replicability. Elise Ince writes about how "It is essential for consumer psychologists to publish robust results that should be easy to replicate." Such replication also relates to what may actually transfer from the lab to the "real" world. Nitika Garg notes that "there is also a shift towards examining issues which have real-world impact." While these new developments are happening, some also caution that the fundamental goals of consumer psychology should not get lost. In the words of David Brinberg, "I hope the field returns to asking and addressing important theoretical questions that examine important social/consumer problems..." But our panelists also express considerable optimism for the future. Jesse Itzkowitz states that "The field is wide open," Nitika Garg mentions "I am excited about some of the more recent shifts in the field" and Priyali Rajagopal aptly concludes as follows: "I believe that the future of consumer psychology is bright. While specific research topics that will be viewed as interesting or important will continue to evolve as consumers and their consumption practices evolve, the study of consumers will remain critically important to marketers, public policy makers and consumers themselves."

CONCLUSION

We, the authors, have truly enjoyed our careers in consumer psychology and hope that this book plays a role in motivating you to give serious consideration to this career, and in providing a way forward. Whether you follow the academic path of consumer psychology—the one that the two of us chose—or the non-academic path that so many others follow, trying to understand the mind of a consumer is a genuinely fascinating endeavor. After all, given that each of us is a consumer of goods and services in the world, understanding the psychology of consumers is a step toward understanding oneself. Wish you all the best!

Appendix: Verbatim Responses of Several Consumer Psychologists

A. WHY I THINK OF MYSELF AS A CONSUMER PSYCHOLOGIST

Survey Responses to the Following Question:

Why do you think of yourself as a consumer psychologist? (Please write about what you do, and which elements of your job relate to being a consumer psychologist.)

1. *Wilson Bastos*:

   I see myself primarily as a Marketing academic. At the "core", however, I am someone interested in understanding the psychology of the consumer. And I do relate more to the second than the first. I also feel more proud of saying that I study the consumer than marketing in general. Perhaps because we, as a community, have not marketed marketing well enough to convey its benefits to society, leading to the stigmas often associated with "marketing".

   My research focuses on how the material versus experiential purchases categorization can predict psychological benefits (e.g., happiness) and various forms of consumer behaviors (e.g., WOM, reaction to a price increase).

2. *Kerry Bianchi*:

   Thinking broadly about consumer psychology as a study of customer behavior, thought, action, emotion and reaction is intrinsically linked to advertising, where I've spent much of my career. The goal of any marketer is to elicit a response from a consumer—perhaps first as brand awareness, then affinity or interest, and hopefully eventually as action or engagement. Finding the right combination of messaging, content, design, delivery and context are all important variables that impact advertising effectiveness. In my current role, we have built software to help enterprises buy and evaluate their digital advertising to see how effective different ads, targeting methods, geographies, formats and screens, ad inventory, etc. impact performance, as well as which audiences respond the best.

3. *David Brinberg*:
   I do not categorize myself as a consumer psychologist, but as an applied social psychologist interested in decision making, social issues, dyadic and small group behavior, and research methodology. I think my interests align with research areas in consumer psychology, but not exclusively in that domain.

4. *Kristina Durante*:
   I consider myself a consumer psychologist because the outcomes that I measure are related to or directly involve purchase decisions and preferences. I also consider myself a consumer psychologist because I experimentally manipulate the environments in which people are making consumer decisions in order to measure how these manipulated factors can change purchase decisions.

5. *David Gal*:

    I try to understand behavior. Though most of my work is based on experiments, as I've matured in my career, I've become less tied to methodology and more focused on using any method ('anything goes' in the words of the philosopher of science Paul Feyerabend) to understand behavior. This includes surveys, critical observation and analysis, secondary data, self-report data, analytical models, and so forth.

6. *Nitika Garg*:

    Because as a researcher, I am interested in understanding why consumers do what they do, their motivations and emotions, and how these impact their behavior.

7. *Abhijit Guha*:

    Academic researcher, studying consumer behavior. I teach consumer behavior (undergraduates/ PhD) and I research consumer behavior (specifically, issues re. pricing).

8. *Paul Herr*:

    I study consumption and its antecedents (and occasionally, consequences) using techniques developed by psychologists, within frameworks developed by psychologists, and interpret relevant data through the lens of social and cognitive psychology. (I don't think of myself exclusively, or even very often, as a consumer psychologist. I do consider myself a marketer whose training in social psychology provides insight into interesting marketing phenomena.)

9. *Elise Ince*:

Mainly because of the research I do (my teaching is quite different). In my research, I bring light on the psychological processes that explain the different effects I am studying. At the same time, I also continuously question and analyze my environment, as well as my interactions with others, to look for interesting effects to study or answers to questions I have.

10. *Mathew Isaac*:

I study how consumers make judgments and decisions and I try to understand how psychological processes (e.g., perception, categorization, etc.) affect these judgments and decisions.

11. *Jesse Itzkowitz*:

There are three aspects to my job as a behavioral scientist at Ipsos. The first is serving as a thought leader and evangelist for the application of rigorous academic frameworks and methodologies to business challenges—both within my own organization and within the market research industry. The second aspect is to help my company optimize their current market research offerings to be in line with best-practices from academia and to develop new products and methods based on peer-reviewed and validated techniques. The final aspect, and the one

where I spend most of my time, is helping our array
of Fortune 100 clients use behavioral science to help
identify and influence the nonconscious factors
that drive consumer goals, consumer beliefs, and
ultimately—consumer decisions.

12. *Carl Marci*:

I was founder of one of the first consumer
neuroscience firms in the world. https://en.wikipedia.
org/wiki/Innerscope_Research. As a founder and
CEO, we developed tools that took neuroscience
and related physiological measures to marketing and
media companies to get new and deeper insights into
consumers emotional responses. I am author of 6 US
patents and the company was acquired by Nielsen
in 2015. As Chief Neuroscientist, I oversee the
messaging and product development for our division,
which has offices in 8 countries.

13. *Steve Neumann*:

A consumer psychologist is obsessed with
understanding why people do the things they do
when exploring and making purchase choices for
goods and services and what they think and how they
behave afterwards. This describes the 'red thread'
that has woven its way through my entire career as
a consumer researcher and a marketer and has been
at the center of what I do. Most recently, the vast
majority of my job was ensuring that my team of
consumer research professionals and I lived, slept

and breathed what drives consumers to make the choices they do and then look for the insight ... that deep understanding that the Company can use for competitive advantage.

14. *Priyali Rajagopal*:
    I study the psychology of consumption specifically with respect to consumer information processing and memory. Thus, my research interests, the domains and contexts that I research all pertain to consumers and their psychology.

15. *Jose Ribas Fernandes*:
    I am an associate at an applied behavioral science management consulting company, using an evidence-based approach, and if possible empirical, to redesign services to improve decision making. Consumer psychology is one of the sources of theories and evidence that I draw from as a practitioner (others being social and cognitive psychology, and behavioral economics). My mental framework, from my graduate training, borders consumer psychology. I identify more as an applied scientist of decision making where choices, broadly defined, are the unit of analysis. Of these choices, those pertaining to acquisition, usage, and disposal of goods, are a subset of my focus.

16. *Ritesh Saini*:
    As a researcher and teacher.

17. *Neela Saldanha*:

    All marketing problems are fundamentally consumer psychology problems and since I work in marketing, I think of myself as a consumer psychologist.

    At the Centre, we work on behaviour change programmes. For example, a programme we are working on is to improve adherence among pregnant women for iron and folic acid supplements to reduce anemia and therefore improve maternal and child health. While the tablets are available for free, people still don't use them consistently. Why? Uncovering barriers and designing programmes to address these barriers is a challenging and enjoyable exercise.

    One of the key things I've noticed in the social sector is that we don't think of low-income communities as "consumers". We prefer to call them "beneficiaries." But this downplays the freedom of choice that they have—even if that choice is not to adopt a free product or service. I would like to see more of a consumer-oriented mindset in the social sector.

    We use behavioural science (blend of social psychology, behavioural economics, consumer psychology) to help design programmes.

18. *Gulen Sarial Abi*:

    Division 23 of APA, the Divison of Consumer Psychology, suggests that consumer psychology employs theoretical psychological approaches to understanding consumers. Hence, a consumer psychologist is a scholar, who employs theoretical psychological approaches to understanding consumers. I define myself as a consumer psychologist because in my research, I also employ theoretical psychological approaches to understanding consumers.

In general, I try to explain the behavior of consumers when they experience psychological threats. More specifically, I investigate the effects of financial restrictions and other psychological threats (e.g., mortality threats) on consumer behavior (e.g., their attitudes towards brands, their preferences of certain product types). I try to understand the psychological processes behind the effects of psychological threats on consumer behavior. Hence, I think that I am a consumer psychologist.

19. *Julio Sevilla*:
    I do research to try to understand how consumers make decisions, so I delve into the psychological processes people go through when they act as consumers.

20. *Antonios Stamatogiannakis*:
    I think my most indicative characteristic as a consumer psychologist relates to my life in general, not so much to my job. Specifically, I often find myself wondering why consumers like (or dislike) something, why they buy (or don't buy) things, why they use (or don't use) what they own and so on.

These questions are largely a natural impulse I have. My job gives me the training and the resources to study this natural impulse systematically.

21. *Stephanie Tully*:
The research portion of my position requires me to be a consumer psychologist. All of my research is spent hypothesizing and testing theories about how consumers behave and testing these theories empirically.

22. *Dengfeng Yan*:
Most of my research is focused on understanding the psychology underlying consumer reactions to marketing mix such as prices, packages, promotions, and so on.

23. *Meng Zhu*:
I study human judgment and decision making, employing the paradigms from both behavioral economics and classic psychology. I try to understand the psychology of consumer, as humans.

B. HOW I BECAME A CONSUMER PSYCHOLOGIST

Survey Responses to the Following Question:

How did you end up becoming a consumer psychologist? (Please write about how your education and/or your career trajectory led you to becoming a consumer psychologist.)

1. *Wilson Bastos*:
   Upon entering the PhD program I knew I had an interest in people (vs. firms or other agents of the marketplace), but I barely knew the difference between being a consumer psychologist versus a "CCT" scholar. In an informal conversation with Paul Connell, then a senior PhD student at the University of Arizona, he explained to me what it was like to do a minor in psychology. I thought: This is IT! So I went for it. Along the way I was fortunate to be taught by amazing professors (e.g., Merrie Brucks, Linda Price, Melanie Wallendorf, Matthias Mehl, Jeff Stone, Jeff Greenberg) who enabled me to understand the person from both a broad and a focused viewpoint.

2. *Kerry Bianchi:*
   I was a psychology major and did my senior thesis on the topic of gender roles in advertising. I knew I was interested in advertising and took an entry level job at an advertising agency directly out of college. From there, I had the opportunity to explore advertising and the psychology of consumers from a number of different marketing and advertising related roles—at media companies; in a global management consulting firm; as part of advertising technology enterprises; and also leading customer acquisition for a financial services company focused on online trading.

3. *David Brinberg*:

   I do not feel I have become a consumer psychologist.
   My career trajectory reflects areas of interest and
   research collaborations that were often fortuitous. For
   example, I met a FDA researcher, Louis Morris, while
   at the University of Maryland and conducted the early
   research with him on defining direct to consumer
   advertising of prescription drugs that helped to define
   the regulatory framework for these promotional efforts.
   I met an assistant professor in Food and Nutrition at
   the University of Maryland, which led to a lifetime of
   research on food-choice and food-related behavior. At
   Virginia Tech, I created a Sloan Foundation funded
   industry center that focused forest-related products
   and economic development. My research interests over
   time reflect finding smart people with interesting ideas,
   and exploring conceptual frameworks and substantive
   problems of mutual interest.

4. *Kristina Durante*:

   I was working in entertainment marketing (in
   industry) and took some psychology courses (while
   working) to learn more about consumer persuasion.
   I then became interested in tackling research questions
   head-on and eventually entered a PhD program in
   psychology. Although I was in a psychology program,
   my research involved consumer decisions. Having
   no formal guidance when choosing PhD programs,
   I didn't realize that a PhD in marketing was aligned
   with the outcomes I was interested in studying.

In industry we did not consider the many factors that might influence consumers differently from year to year, day to day, or even moment to moment. We only considered what we did last year when we had a similar product entering the marketplace. It was exciting to be able to enhance the marketing process by incorporating a stronger understanding of how the mind works.

5. *David Gal*:
    Like a lot of naïve youth I, for a while, imagined myself changing the world. With a computer science undergraduate degree, and while pursuing a 1 year masters in management science & engineering at Stanford, I started to think practically, however, about what was next. I didn't have much interest in returning to the corporate world (I had previously worked at Capital One and some startups over a 2 year period), and I thought I might apply for an MBA program. But I had two roommates that were enrolled in PhD programs, one in computer science and the other in economics. It seemed like a good lifestyle of sleeping in and getting paid to think (waking up early was the worst part of corporate life for me). I enrolled in Itamar Simonson's PhD class in behavioral decision making and thought it was a lot of fun, and couldn't believe people were getting paid (and well) to think about why people behaved the way they do. Dan Ariely was sitting in on the class—he had long pink hair at the time—and I thought that

if a Professor at MIT could have long pink hair and be a star in the field it was the kind of career path that lent itself to noncomformity—which was something that highly appealed to me.

6. *Nitika Garg*:
   I did my BSc in Computer Science and I always knew that I would follow it up with an MBA. While doing my MBA, I realised that I enjoyed Marketing the most as a subject and that is what I ended up majoring in. During MBA, I also got interested in pursuing PhD and thus, when I graduated, I joined the PhD program in Marketing. It was a sort of a natural progression for me where once I became aware of the specialisations within Marketing research, I was drawn to consumer psychology and consumer behavior.

7. *Abhijit Guha*:
   The PhD program at Duke sparked my interest in consumer behavior.

8. *Paul Herr*:
   Took a post doc and then tenure track assistant professor position at Carnegie-Mellon University out of (a) curiosity, and (b) because choice and consumption are perfect domains for studying cognitive psychology in the "real" world– for instance, new and evolving categories and category structure, learning of meaningful new objects (as opposed to meaningless nonsense syllables) and so on.

9. *Elise Ince*:

I came to marketing by a process of elimination within business (having studied accounting, finance and marketing, I knew I didn't prefer the first two) and chose consumer psychology also by elimination within marketing. However, in retrospect, my selection by rejection was simply due to my ignorance. I only knew marketing as a managerial topic. Had I known more about consumer psychology, I would have selected it right away as it is a perfect fit for my innate curiosity about people and decision making in general.

10. *Mathew Isaac*:

I became interested in consumer psychology when I was working (post-MBA) for a management consulting firm, Bain & Company. My clients were often private equity firms that asked us to conduct "strategic due diligence" to understand the future prospects of industries in which they were considering investing. To do this, we often conducted in-depth interviews with prospective and current customers. I remember being fascinated by the way in which consumers, particularly in retail categories, made their purchase decisions because they seemed highly irrational. I was intrigued by the psychological factors that led people to buy or not buy. While at Bain, I decided to apply to PhD programs in Marketing. I was also indirectly influenced to become a professor by my father, who was a business professor.

10. *Jesse Itzkowitz*:

    I've always been interested in decision making.
    When my academic job moved from a scholarly one
    to a teaching one, I needed a change. This was that
    change.

12. *Carl Marci*:

    I have two degrees in psychology and a medical
    degree with post-graduate training in psychiatry.
    I was collaborating with faculty and students at the
    MIT Media Lab and was approached by a business
    student to take some of the technology I was using
    in depression research and apply it to consumer
    psychology. We started Innerscope Research
    in 2006.

13. *Steve Neumann*:

    I started my career while in post-graduate studies
    conducting door to door interviews with consumers.
    This gave me a first hand view of human behavior
    and fueled my interest in what drives consumer
    decisions. My favorite post-graduate courses were
    those from the business college focused on consumer
    behavior and from the journalism-advertising
    department where I was able to apply the principles
    in the creation of consumer communications. Post
    college, I went to work in the research department
    of advertising agencies. At that time, agencies still
    handled a lot of the consumer research for their
    clients and were leading a lot of the thinking in
    the industry. I quickly learned that if one wanted

to be successful in the discipline, it was imperative to develop a comprehensive understanding of why consumers behave the way they do. What wants and needs do they have? Which of those are met and unmet? What are their attitudes and beliefs and how do those impact their choices? I also came to learn that while you can delegate data collection and study conduct to third party research companies, it is imperative that you have a personal curiosity that lets you watch people shop, ask friends and family why they made the choices they did and take a personal approach. The best consumer psychologists I have known have this personal interest and drive.

14. *Priyali Rajagopal*:

As a product manager in India, I quickly realized that the aspect of my job that most appealed to me was marketing research, specifically the generation of consumer insights. I was fascinated by how these insights were generated, and wanted to learn more about why consumers held the beliefs that they did and why they had the specific consumption patterns that our research uncovered. However, I noted that research which had useful and immediate application from a marketing strategy/tactical standpoint was valued and prioritized over the understanding of deeper psychological insights whose immediate utility to marketing was not readily apparent. This gap led me to consider a doctorate in consumer psychology.

15. *Jose Ribas Fernandes*:

    For the last decade I have worked as a cognitive neuroscientist working on the neural mechanisms of human decision making at first as a PhD student, and then as a post-doc, at research institutions. In the last years, I felt a yearning to use academic knowledge on decision making to solve applied problems, rather than theoretical. I felt that publishing was not impactful enough, despite it being the gold standard for academic impact.

    I looked for companies working on applied behavioral economics, since it was one of the most burgeoning fields of application. I started working at BEworks about a year ago, where the approach is very similar to studying working memory or any other theoretical constructs drawing from published academic research, and with a focus on conducting experiments.

16. *Ritesh Saini*:

    Was interested in psychology since late teens. Saw an interesting synergy of psychology in marketing during my MBA. Have been interested in how consumers make decisions ever since.

17. *Neela Saldanha*:

    After a BA in Economics, I went in for an MBA course because it was the most practical thing to do (I wasn't sure of how an MA in Economics trajectory would work out, practically). I enjoyed marketing,

and disliked finance (the two main streams) so that
was that, really. I really enjoyed my summer training
at Unilever where I had to uncover insights and
design a positioning strategy for a detergent. I found
I had a knack for this. My early career was a series of
half-thought out choices dictated by a mix of interests
(I joined Bestfoods from Nestle because it was doing
amazing work in overturning a market leader i..e
Maggi through Knorr), cities (Delhi to Mumbai)
and money.

While I was at Accenture, consulting with clients
on marketing strategies, I realized that most of my
recommendations were anecdotal. I was searching
for more rigorous theory driven routes to apply
marketing and found that all of them were in
academic papers. So I applied to do a PhD and got in.
But I soon realized I didn't want to pursue academic
marketing—but rather apply all the cool theories
people were developing to real problems and seeing
what stuck.

So, after the PhD, I joined PepsiCo in New York,
worked there for seven years and two years ago,
got a call from the head of the Gates Foundation in
India about this exciting opportunity to use good
marketing for social impact. So here I am!

18. *Gulen Sarial Abi*:
    I had my Bachelor of Arts degree in Business
    Administration from Koc University in Turkey in

2003. During my junior year, I took the Consumer Behavior elective course. It was the first time that I was exposed to consumer behavior research. I remember doing different research projects trying to understand how consumers behave in the marketplace.

After my undergraduate degree, I pursued my Master of Science degree in Management Research at Said Business School, University of Oxford. My major was in marketing, where I wrote my MSc thesis on consumers' perceptions of local and global retailers in Turkey. During my MSc degree, I was also exposed to different research methods. For example, for my qualitative research methods course, being a Muslim, I spent my Sundays in church gatherings in order to investigate the effect of religion on behavior by doing an ethnographic research. All these experiences influenced my curiosity to investigate how consumers behave in the marketplace.

I should admit that I had no real idea what becoming a consumer psychologist really means before meeting with Prof. Zeynep Gurhan Canli at Koc University, Turkey. I pursued my PhD in Business Administration under the supervision of Zeynep Gurhan Canli, who really taught me everything about becoming a consumer psychologist. While I thought that doing a PhD in marketing was mainly about branding or company strategies, I have learnt how scholars can employ different theoretical psychological approaches to understanding consumers. My knowledge and fascination with the field of consumer psychology extended when I spent a year at Stanford Graduate School of Business as a visiting scholar. Working with Prof. Christian Wheeler and Prof. Baba Shiv as well as taking the PhD level course from Stanford University's psychology department really taught me what it really means to be a consumer psychologist. As a result of all my education and the people that I had the chance to work with, I ended up becoming a consumer psychologist.

19. *Julio Sevilla*:
    My background is in engineering and I subsequently did an MBA. I really liked my Marketing classes during the program and decided I wanted to be an academic and dig deeper into Marketing, specifically, Consumer Behavior.

20. *Antonios Stamatogiannakis*:
    Since I remember myself I always tried to understand why people behave the way they do—which already made me an intuitive psychologist from a very young age. I might have studied psychology from the very beginning, but in Greece the opportunities for studying social, cognitive, or consumer psychology were non-existent when I started my studies So I started studying business disciplines (management, marketing), mostly because I found a general interest in these topics. During my studies, I used something like an implicit funnel to end up in consumer psychology: First, I realized I did not like accounting/

finance. Then I started finding general management boring. So I focused on marketing. And after ruling out several disciplines of marketing (strategy, B2B etc.), I understood that really wanted to study consumers.

21. *Stephanie Tully*:

While working after college, I found myself continuing to learn about consumer psychology through pop books on the subject for fun. Given this intrinsic interest, I began to explore degree programs and careers that centered on the topic. My mother found a website for a school's Ph.D. program for marketing and emailed it to me. After looking at the website, I immediately knew that was what I wanted to do with my life.

22. *Dengfeng Yan*:

I was fascinated by branding strategies when I was an undergraduate student. During that time, companies like P&G and Unilever had very high visibility in universities (such as promotions, talks, recruiting, etc.).

23. *Meng Zhu*:

It is through a series of pure randomness. But if I were asked to choose the major again, I might still pick this one, but then I would take more hardcore quant classes during my PhD. As I wish I have the ability to model more complicated decision making problems and analyze more large-scale datasets in order to better quantify human behaviors and predict their future behavioral tendency.

C. WHAT I LIKE AND DISLIKE ABOUT BEING A CONSUMER PSYCHOLOGIST

Survey Responses to the Following Question:

What do you like and dislike about being a consumer psychologist? (Please write about what you enjoy about studying consumers, and if there are particular challenges that are associated with being a consumer psychologist.)

1. *Wilson Bastos*:

LIKE:

(a) Being able to understand why and when (we like to call that mediators and moderators, don't we?) people do what they do is simply amazing! In my first years into the PhD program, Melanie Wallendorf told me that they would give me an additional pair of glasses to see the world. She was so right! The world just seems more colorful and interesting.

(b) Us, as a community. Going to conferences and seeing friends is something I look forward to every year.

(c) It is rewarding to think that, albeit very modestly, the findings of my research can make people's lives better.

(d) The intellectual engagement. Although the review process is sometimes brutal and even inefficient, I am a stronger believer in it. And, believe me,

I enjoy trying to find solutions to reviewers concerns. I especially enjoy the exchanges via the revision notes. It feels like a negotiation of the intellect.

DISLIKE:

The pressure involved in pursuing tenure.

2. *Kerry Bianchi*:

   I think the study of human behavior is endlessly fascinating. And with the multiplicity of formats we can now use to "touch" consumers through physical, digital and virtual environments, there is more to learn every day as consumers interact with products and services in new and innovative ways. With marketing becoming more data driven in the way advertising can be targeted and delivered, there is both a benefit in terms of being able to quantify much more of what happens in consumer marketing, but an equal challenge in trying to decipher which of the many levers ultimately led to the desired action in order to replicate it in the future.

3. *David Brinberg*:

   See my earlier answers.

4. *Kristina Durante*:

   I like almost all aspects of the process of studying consumer psychology. Creating knowledge is truly entrepreneurial and I appreciate that. The art of selling your science for peer review is what I dislike the most.

5. *David Gal*:

   I enjoy thinking about problems. I find it very intellectually stimulating to try to understand a particular behavior and to generate hypotheses and design studies to investigate them.

   The publication process can be frustrating. I particularly get frustrated by my perception that reviewers are fairly rigid in what they view as good methodology. They seem to me to value adherence to study design norms over a focus on using whatever tools are available, despite limitations, to provide understanding. There also seems to me to be a focus on methodological "correctness" over importance.

6. *Nitika Garg*:

   I really enjoy thinking about the psychology that leads to specific consumer behaviors and disentangling the process that motivates those behaviors. Designing experiments that are neat and natural to answer these questions is another thing that I like a lot. One challenge I find with experimental research though is striking the balance between internal and external validity. The latter is critical for gaining insights that are relevant in the real-world but that is a bit of a struggle with this methodology.

7. *Abhijit Guha*:

   Understanding consumers is important, to businesses and policy makers. Hence I feel what I do is important—both in terms of research, and in terms of communicating such knowledge to business students, managers.

Some challenges relate to: (i) not extrapolating from own behavior (I am also a consumer!), (ii) eliciting responses from consumers that they may not wish to reveal/ eliciting responses about subconscious behaviors, and (iii) trying to predict consumer responses to things they may not have thought about e.g. AI.

8. *Paul Herr*:
   Like the ability to address really interesting phenomena of which there are no shortage. Dislike the structure of academic marketing/ consumer psychology in which heuristic processing (department affiliation) rather than merit of ideas/ evidence often determines voice in discipline. The field moves slowly and often in wrong directions, with little regard for method and rigor. Shiny objects (cute phenomena) attract a lot of attention without the systematic examination of the underlying process(es) that illuminate (explain, etc.) the phenomena. Pretty much a complete absence of tying constructs together in meaningful ways that build a productive science, rather than a willy-nilly race to publish as many disparate phenomenon-based demonstration papers.

9. *Elise Ince*:
   I particularly enjoy discovering processes hidden behind people's decision making. I enjoy that

I can relate to the situations I study, being myself a consumer. I also enjoy explaining to others (be it in mundane conversations or when working with Master or doctoral students) all the biases we are prone to. This is because one doesn't need proprietary knowledge about consumer psychology to understand the issue at hand and to participate in the discussion. This doesn't mean there isn't any knowledge to acquire about the topic but discussions are more easily accessible than for other subjects such as accounting or finance. I also enjoy that research is feasible with very little means (no need to pay for expensive databases, software or hardware). In other words, consumer psychology is easily accessible to most audiences.

A challenge specific to consumer psychology is making sure we discover robust effects that replicate.

Although I am more familiar with the quantitative research side of consumer psychology, I would prefer if the field were more open to the qualitative research side as well.

10. *Mathew Isaac*:

I love the process of identifying a heuristic or bias that people unwittingly use to make judgments that seems to be irrational. It's especially gratifying when I am able to uncover a decision bias that is incredibly robust, because I want my work to be replicable and believable, but still "surprising" (at least to some extent). I love running experiments, analyzing data, and writing/ positioning the work against the existing literature. I even enjoy the review process and take pride in being able to convince a review team about the merits of my findings.

I dislike the length of time that it takes for a project to go from idea generation to publication. I also find that some people in the field of consumer research try to overcomplicate things—I have little patience for 2 x 2 x 2 x 2 studies! I also dislike the fact that people assume that the value of consumer research is determined solely by external validity. There is value in theory testing, even if it only applicable in a narrow set of situations in the "real world."

11. *Jesse Itzkowitz*:

I love helping my clients explore their challenges and opportunities in new ways. Businesses are really smart and are often able to find success, but don't always understand the reasons why a particular brand strategy or creative execution "worked." Behavioral science gives them the "why", which they can then use to replicate success in analogous situations and modify their approach to ones that differ significantly.

12. *Carl Marci*:

I very much like helping our clients understand the role of emotion in decision making and helping to make advertising and other brand communications more effective. It is a fast paced industry and we have a lot of fun. I dislike the rapid changes and lack of sophistication of many people in the industry. Traditional marketing training lacks a neuroscience perspective.

13. *Steve Neumann*:

What I like about consumer psychology is that the work is never complete. Just when you think you understand the attitudes that might be influencing behavior, the consumer does something surprising. Applying the work of Kahneman and others and the increasing focus on heuristics has helped to explain these variances, but synthesis, interpretation and insights are still a blend of art and science.

One thing that bothers me is the descriptor "consumer" which has come under some fire for dehumanizing the behavior of people. However, I am uncertain of a better descriptor for the subject of our studies. I have tried terms like "the people we serve" but it seems somewhat vague.

Another thing that bothers me is that there are some marketers who believe that because they have conducted an ethnographic study or some other face to face interaction with consumers that they deeply understand and can predict their behavior. Being a consumer psychologist is a life-long journey and no event or sets of events can provide perfect perspective.

Finally, there are some research suppliers who have developed an approach to understanding consumers.

In many cases, these are valuable tools to help complete the picture, but there are a few of these companies who tout their method as the only way or single best way to gain understanding.

14. *Priyali Rajagopal:*

LIKE:

- It may sound like a cliche—but getting paid quite generously to do what I love to do is one of the best aspects of this profession.
- The research process—having the ability to get answers to any questions that I have on consumer psychology is very rewarding
- Flexibility in work schedule and being able to have a great work-life balance
- Teaching and mentoring students

DISLIKE:

- The publication process:) It took me a while to realize that research and publication are two different processes that require very different skill sets. While having an article published is extremely rewarding, the publication process itself (long timelines, critical review process) is not an enjoyable one.
- This profession tends to be overwhelmingly negative in terms of feedback and outcomes. Thus, good journals have very low acceptance rates, thus leading to many more negative than positive outcomes in terms of publications. The review

process tends to be dauntingly and hauntingly negative and critical! Student evaluations of teaching tend to be critical and negative very often. Hence, it is critically important to be emotionally resilient and persistent in order to be successful and happy as a behavioral scientist/educator.

15. *Jose Ribas Fernandes*:

I enjoy the fact that consumer psychologists have dedicated themselves to understand ecological behavior, and be theoretically rigorous about consumption. I also like the fact that consumer psychologists have had to study choices that are inherently complex. In contrast, most of the work in cognitive psychology and neuroscience, my fields of training, have often eschewed complexity of the decisions being studied for the sake of experimental control. On the other hand, I wonder if the distinction between consumption-related choices and other types of choices is theoretically important. While it has economic importance to study the antecedents of constructs such as brand loyalty, I wonder if it yields an unnecessary duplication from studying non-consumption related types of choices.

16. *Ritesh Saini*:

LIKE:

There are always interesting research questions to ask and answer.

DISLIKE:

- Absence of unifying frameworks in the study of CP.
- Disconnect from the industry/public-policy.

- Methodological isolation (experimentalists don't talk to empiricists).

17. *Neela Saldanha*:

I enjoy thinking about why people might want to do something and especially all the counter-intuitive reasons that they may not.

I enjoy applying theory to practice, to look at a phenomenon and try to label it, and to apply good frameworks to thinking.

I think too much of consumer psychology is still about WEIRD countries (western, educated, industrialized, rich, democratic) and there is very little resonance to countries like India. We don't even have local language for most of the behavioural science terms!

I also wish more consumer psychologists moved out of doing lab studies and doing real-life field studies, the way that the economists run RCTs. It may give a very helpful understanding of the contexts of different field situations.

I dislike that I don't have a community to draw on as someone who is trying to apply behavioural science principles in the social sector—most consumer psychologists are in the US universities and cater to richer populations. Understanding the consumption choices of the poor would be wonderful.

18. *Gulen Sarial Abi*:

I love being a consumer psychologist. First, it helps me to explain my behaviors in the marketplace. I cannot say that I can always apply what I know in terms of consumer behavior in my own behavior but I really love being able to explain why I behave or do not behave in a certain way in the marketplace. Second, consumer psychology is an area where there are limitless research opportunities. Every individual is a consumer and we are all different. This means that we all behave differently. For me, being able to investigate why people behave or do not behave in a certain way is fascinating. Moreover, although I still have to improve a lot, the fact that my research findings might have public policy implications or implications for the general welfare of the society makes me really happy.

I think the major challenge associated with being a consumer psychologist is related with the fact that what we do is pretty much related with psychology. While scholars in psychology do support each other a lot and they are able to publish even the incremental contributions to the existing literature in psychology, often times, scholars in our field do not see the contributions that we make to the consumer psychology literature.

Moreover, unlike psychology where scholars work in big teams, in our field, most of the papers are written by a team of 2–3 scholars. If the different research areas in consumer psychology are dominated by these 2–3 scholars, I feel like it being very difficult to enter into these group of researchers and publish my research.

19. *Julio Sevilla*:
   I like the flexibility and freedom of deciding what topics and research questions I want to study and to be able to decide how I want to approach it. I also enjoy sharing my knowledge with students and the opportunity to play an important role in their professional and personal foundation. The challenge some business academics face and that we should tackle more strongly is that of having closer ties to industry so that it better informs what we study but also that we have the relationships to use these resources to make our research better and more relevant.

20. *Antonios Stamatogiannakis*:
   The best thing is that I can mentally challenge myself about understanding virtually any behavior that I see in my everyday life. The tough part is to find explanations that are considered 'interesting' by today's standards.

21. *Stephanie Tully*:
   I love theory creation, designing studies, and analyzing data. The only part I do not love is the

review process. Though I do think overall the peer review process is helpful and has improved my research in many cases, this is not always true and it can be frustrating at times when reviewers try to take your work in different directions.

22. *Dengfeng Yan*:

I can freely explore whatever research idea that intrigues me. I also enjoy observing consumer behaviors in the real marketplace and see how people behave differently and how their behaviors change over time.

In terms of challenges, I guess sometimes it's difficult to know what really drives consumer purchases. Fortunately, new methods such as eye-tracking and brain imaging are developed to help us better understand consumers.

23. *Meng Zhu*:

I enjoy studying human, not necessarily consumers. But good thing is that any human is perhaps a consumer. I don't like being limited to study coupons when I can work on a much broader and more impactful issue. But I do think many of our work has direct implications for humans, as consumers (but the findings/implications have to be insightful enough rather than cheap sentences). And it is good to feel that our work might produce difference in the real marketplaces that are sizable.

D. WHAT ADVICE I HAVE FOR THOSE CONSIDERING CONSUMER PSYCHOLOGY

Survey Responses to the Following Question:

What advice would you give to someone who would want to become a consumer psychologist of the kind that you are? (Please write about what kind of education and/or career moves would help someone become a consumer psychologist of your kind.)

1. *Wilson Bastos*:
   Read broadly and deeply. Accept the reality that you are often wrong in your thinking, and seek the truth. In your everyday life, be conscious about what's going on around you. Research ideas will pop up all the time. Listen attentively to what people say. Whenever something sounds curious, write it down. It might just be an interesting topic to study.

2. *Kerry Bianchi*:
   I think a combination of psychology, marketing, data and technology are all ripe areas for study that would help make a well rounded consumer psychologist in my field. You need to understand what motivates consumers, which many might first think of as the emotional, visual or logical elements conveyed by a brand but nowadays should also include data, technology and analytics as these are being used more often to both execute AND measure results

of consumer impact. I would also be open minded about career paths—mine was not linear and I think it has been a benefit to see my industry from several different 'seats', providing a more holistic view to approaching consumers and advertising.

3. *David Brinberg:*
   My answer is a bit of a cliché, but also the way I have approached research—be open to the ideas of smart people, find colleagues who you like, enjoy and who you can find laughter with, and spend time simply exploring ideas and problems. An outgrowth of this "wasted time" is often some exciting research.

4. *Kristina Durante:*
   The one thing I would advice someone to do differently than me is enter a marketing PhD program instead of a psychology PhD program.

5. *David Gal:*
   I wouldn't necessarily advise someone to become a consumer psychologist. It is easy to work on a problem for many years without much resolution (and therefore no publication), whereas the academic job market is very competitive and demands consistent publications.

   That said, the path of least resistance to a career as a consumer psychologist is to study psychology and/or economics in undergrad while working as a research assistant for a well-known researcher in the field. An additional year or two of RA work post-undergrad might also be helpful. Of particular importance is generating one's own research hypotheses and testing them. Regardless of the path one chooses prior to applying to a doctoral program in consumer psychology, reading articles in the leading journals in the field (e.g., Journal of Consumer Research) or taking a doctoral level course while in undergrad or a masters program is essential to getting a flavor of the type of work consumer psychologists do.

6. *Nitika Garg*:
   The one advice I would give is that get into this area if you really are curious about why people do what they do and are willing to (often times) grapple with these issues even when the answer might not be obvious. You have to have passion for your area. Do not choose a topic just because it is the "hot" area.

   Finally, gain as much methodological rigor as you can in your training. It will stand you in good stead in your career.

7. *Abhijit Guha*:
   Education helps (Psychology and related degrees). Practical experience also helps (suitable positions in firms/ consulting firms/ research firms/ policy groups). Finally, being curious is an asset.

8. *Paul Herr*:
   Get an advanced degree in psychology. Don't call yourself a consumer psychologist without

having requisite qualifications. Never sacrifice methodological and statistical rigor for expedience. Pick your colleagues carefully. Don't let reviewers and editors dissuade you from directions in which the data lead.

9. *Elise Ince*:
   Be knowledgeable about research in consumer psychology (e.g. reading peer reviewed publications as well as some more mainstream books); master statistics; start early accumulating experience on the subject (e.g. writing an honor thesis; helping a professor do research as a student; spending a year working as a research assistant; and attending specialty conferences). All these are especially important if you consider applying to a PhD program. This is because more and more PhD applicants have experience doing consumer psychology research (often by being part of a research project, having presented at conferences, or even having published a paper).

10. *Mathew Isaac*:
   I became a consumer psychologist as a second career after being a post-MBA strategy consultant for 5 years. Although my "real world" experience allows me to identify problems/questions that may be relevant to managers, the easiest 'path' to become a researcher is to be a Psychology major in college, to work in a lab for a couple of years as a research assistant, and to apply to PhD programs from there.

11. *Jesse Itzkowitz*:

    Get a PhD in marketing. Be fluent in the consumer behavior literature. You need to be able to access and explain ideas ranging from "terror management theory" to "priming" to "addiction". You'll need to be familiar with a large range of methodologies— business is not that used to experimentation and much of current marketing research uses traditional surveys and qualitative techniques (in-depth interviews, focus groups, ethnography). Learn to "talk business". Read, read, read!

12. *Carl Marci*:

    Best route is to get a solid education in psychology and/or neuroscience and then apply for a job at an existing firm for training and to learn the trade. The other path is to complement your education with reading (including the text book from MIT Press, 'Consumer Neuroscience') and join a brand team for a major advertiser and help educate them about consumer psychology.

13. *Steve Neumann*:

    Educationally, I think there are a number of backgrounds that can effectively work to provide the foundation for good consumer psychology— psychology, sociology, anthropology, marketing, advertising and communications just to name a few. However, whatever the core study area, it is imperative to supplement it with courses from the other disciplines. For example, courses in anthropology, psychology and communications would be excellent complements for a marketing or business core. Some colleges offer excellent consumer research curriculums which is a good area of focus, but again supplementing it with course work from psychology or anthropology provides great dimension.

I also recommend volunteering at places where there is a high interaction level with people. For example, soup kitchens expose one to a broad cross-section of people and behaviors. Jobs that have a high interaction with people (barista, store clerk, store door delivery person) or purchases (stocking shelves) also provide an great opportunity for observation. One summer I worked from time to time helping a family friend in a cheese store in my small home town. It was fascinating to see the different purchase patterns by family type, occasion and other characteristics.

Most of all, as I have said earlier, having an insatiable curiosity about why people are making the choices they do is very important. One of my best bosses would publicly criticize market research findings, yet if you ever accompanied him to a store he was the ultimate consumer researcher. He would observe people in-aisle and then engage them in a conversation about why they made the choice they did. He had that desire to understand the "why" behind their behavior.

14. *Priyali Rajagopal*:

    An undergraduate degree in psychology or economics along with some practical exposure to the research process (e.g. working as a student research assistant) would be very helpful in identifying topics/ areas of potential research interest and acquiring important research skills. Developing excellent written and oral communication skills is also important.

15. *Jose Ribas Fernandes*:

    If you have a passion for application and academic rigour, and understanding real-world behavior, I highly recommend becoming a consumer psychologist!

16. *Ritesh Saini*:

    To have a very widespread theoretical education. Big-data collection and analysis expertise.

17. *Neela Saldanha*:

    (a) Explore all paths. (b) Get really good at data science/technical /methods work in school. Hard to pick it up later, so go to the highest level you can find. Everything is becoming analytical now. (c) Learn about digital technologies. (d) Preferably a joint PhD in economics/psychology or decision making but not sure of field interest in social sector. May be easier to in economics (development economics) with a psychology minor.

18. *Gulen Sarial Abi*:

I think in order to answer this question,
I should first define how I see what kind of a
consumer psychologist I am. I am a consumer
psychologist outside of the U.S., who works really
hard to investigate how consumers behave in
the marketplace, who tries to improve herself
methodologically, and who is not very satisfied with
her career comparing the effort she puts on doing
research with her research output.

Being outside of the U.S., I feel like being outside
of the loop although I have many different research
collaborations. I do not have the opportunity to attend
the different marketing research camps organized by
different schools in the U.S. I believe that this is very
important in order to publish our papers. In order
to overcome this obstacle, being in Europe, together
with couple of other scholars, we've been organizing
the Mediterranean Consumer Behavior Symposium
since 2015. I believe that more of these symposiums
or marketing research camps are needed in Europe in
order for the scholars in Europe. Hence, my first advice
would be to either have their PhD in the U.S.—this
is very sad to say, or do a PhD under the supervision
of a professor who is a consumer psychologist in a
university, which has a psychology department.

Being a consumer psychologist, one should definitely
have a fundamental background in psychology.
Hence, if the university you're pursuing your

PhD does not have a psychology department, you should definitely spend some time during your PhD. in a good university that has good psychology department.

I strongly believe that a consumer psychologist should have different tools to investigate the behavior of consumers in the marketplace. In order to have these tools, a consumer psychologist should invest time to learn different methodological approaches to study consumer behavior. There are many different types of data available to understand consumers. One should not only be restricted with the experimental methods. Until I have started to work as Assistant Professor of Marketing at Bocconi University, my knowledge was only limited with experiments. However, I can now analyze the behavior of consumers by analyzing secondary data on consumer finances or extracting consumer communications from social media. I would strongly advice that if you want to become a consumer psychologist, you should not only restrict your research with an experimental method.I think I still do not have an answer to the question of how to become a good consumer psychologist. Looking at my research output, I will probably not be considered as a good consumer psychologist. I try to improve everyday and I believe that my persistence and hard work will payoff one day. Hence, the last advice that I can give might be that there will be times that you'll feel as not being a good consumer psychologist but I think you should show perseverance in investigating how consumers behave in the marketplace.

19. *Julio Sevilla*:
    This is a great career with many rewarding aspects, however, it also involves a full professional commitment so it is good to get informed by using resources such as this and talking to several academics in order to figure out if there is a fit between what the job involves and our particular abilities and preferences. Take your time getting informed and deciding whether to pursue this career to avoid the potential of rushing to a decision to later find out that this path was not a good fit.

20. *Antonios Stamatogiannakis*:
    Study psychology, statistics, and business. The first will help you understand and expand theory. The second, to be methodologically rigorous. The third, to communicate with the diverse stakeholders that you will have to deal with in a business school.

21. *Stephanie Tully*:
    I would tell them that to do well in this career, you have to be passionate about what you do. I would recommend reading a number of books as well as academic papers to see what interests them. Then I would recommend contacting professors doing the type of research they find interesting and trying to gain some research experience—both to put on a CV,

and also to ensure they enjoy conducting research. Then, I would recommend getting into the best Ph.D. program they possibly can.

I also think that working between college and a Ph.D. program is invaluable. It gives you a perspective for how companies operate, what a job in industry is like, etc. I find my work experience to help both in terms of thinking about research questions and problems as well as for teaching and advising students.

22. *Dengfeng Yan*:
    Next time when you watch a show, don't skip the ad.

23. *Meng Zhu*:
    - have good intuitions (if you can't make people understand what you are working on in two sentences, it is your fault, not theirs)

    - be a super active thinker—don't be lazy at all in thinking (most of the time, the additional thinking differentiates good consumer psychologists from mediocre ones)

    - try to stop thinking only when whatever you come up is parsimonious (nothing too complicated is thoughtful enough)

    - try to be persistent (it's a depressing job at the beginning but gets better soon enough) and work hard (nothing worth having comes easy)

- find a core group of similarly minded friends, that matter a lot, a lot.

- be nice to people, as you never know who they are and who they will become

- be sensitive enough so you know what to improve, but don't be too sensitive so that you are incapable of taking risks

- seek feedback from people you trust, but their advices often conflict, so focus on their reasonings instead

- have a life beyond academic, that helps put you in healthier perspectives

- work on timely and interesting topics with a group of nice people together, as negative people kills a field whereas positive people grows a field.

E. HOW I SEE THE FIELD OF CONSUMER PSYCHOLOGY EVOLVING

Survey Responses to the Following Question:

How do you see the field of consumer psychology evolving in the future, and what are the long-term career prospects for a consumer-psychologist? (Please write about how you expect this field to change in the coming years, and the opportunities/ challenges that future consumer psychologists may encounter.)

1. *Wilson Bastos*:

   (a) I believe we are a very small community still. As a result, we can only study a few domains at a time. I hope we grow rapidly in the number of scholars and publication outlets.

   (b) Overall, I have a very optimistic view of where we are going. We have quickly identified problems (e.g., data manipulation), reacted against them, and taken measures to address them. We are also quick in taking advantage of opportunities (e.g., Mturk) and creatively nurturing knowledge creation in our junior members (e.g., workshops at conferences). We do so informally as well, as when the two authors of this book friendly reviewed a paper of mine just a few months ago.

   (c) I expect us to become increasingly more independent from the general discipline of Marketing. This will happen if we can clearly communicate what we are about and society sees us as agents acting for the benefit of the consumer.

2. *Kerry Bianchi*:
   Extracting consumer data will need to keep pace with the new ways we can deliver experiences to consumers. Consumers now wear and carry devices near constantly that can serve to provide data insights as well as delivery mechanisms for consumer messages. How do we continue to execute

marketing in a way that is accepted and valued versus intrusive or ignored? And as we become more data and technology driven, what will the role of humans be in consumer interactions—you see already in some corners a backlash to the abundance of tech and desire for human connection, what impact will that have on consumer psychology? One thing is for certain, there will be no shortage of roles that require a deep understanding of consumer psychology and the constant changes in how to connect with consumers means there will be need for constant innovation, development and insight in this field.

3. *David Brinberg*:
   I hope the field returns to asking and addressing important theoretical questions that examine important social / consumer problems rather that the rather formulaic approach of 3–4 studies that examine a "counter-intuitive" effect.

4. *Kristina Durante*:
   The biggest challenge might be in the classroom as everything moves digital. It's uncertain the impact this might have.

   This also offers some opportunity for research. The digital landscape we know today happened so quickly that researchers are just beginning to scratch the surface of what it means to engage consumers who are at once seamlessly traceable, but painfully inundated with persuasive messaging.

5. *David Gal*:

   My perception is that the field is getting more competitive and that the demand for publications is correspondingly increasing. I don't think this is necessarily good for the field as it can focus researchers on low-risk, formulaic projects with an easier path to publication. Nonetheless, I don't want to be too negative, I think there remains a strong appreciation in consumer psychology research—probably more so than in other areas of psychology—for original ideas and unconventional work. Moreover, I sense that many people in the field share my view that a lot of research in the field has become too formulaic and predictable, and, therefore, the value attached to work that takes a different approach or tackles more unique or deeper problems is likely to grow.

6. *Nitika Garg*:

   I am excited by some of the more recent shifts in the field. For one, we are becoming more aware of the need for replication, robustness or findings, and overall, transparency of method. Second, there is also a shift towards examining issues which have real-world impact. We need more on both issues but I think we are making good progress in these areas.

7. *Abhijit Guha*:

   Big data/ AI/ iOT will allow for us to study consumer behavior in various ways, but pulling insight from such large and diverse amounts of data is/ will be very complicated. Consumer psychologists will need to extend their investigations into this domain, which is often outside existing skill set.

In my opinion, two issues will emerge as very important in the days ahead. The first relates to privacy in an age of big data etc. The second relates to managing the interface between robots and humans, in an age where robots will slowly become more "human-like". Consumer psychologists are well equipped to lead investigations in these areas, a major opportunity.

7. *Paul Herr:*

I expect the discipline will become more analytics-based (in the narrow sense of the term) without a concurrent increase in conceptual understanding.

8. *Elise Ince:*

Online panels have open new horizons for the field of consumer psychology, making it easier, faster and cheaper to collect data and thus boosting research productivity. It has also increased accessibility to the field in general to those institutions or individuals who did not have access to a behavioral laboratory to collect data. New technologies, or access to these technologies (such as eye tracking, facial recognition, EEG, EMG together with other biometric sensors) and possibly virtual reality, are widening this horizon, as these technologies will help answer questions that are still left open.

The main challenge is the replicability crisis facing consumer psychology. It is essential for consumer psychologists to publish robust results that should be easy to replicate. This issue is affecting how people outside the field judge consumer psychology and can tarnish its reputation. It is therefore important to keep the discussion open among all members and decide how best to face this issue. This will probably lead to important changes in the near future. However what those changes will be is not clear yet.

10. *Mathew Isaac*:

    I think the question of transparency and replicability will continue to come up. Consumer psychologists will be expected to show both robustness and external validity in the same paper, and they will probably be required to pre-register and share all data/stimuli for their experiments. Also, even larger and more diverse samples (e.g., not mTurk only) will be required. This is probably a good change for the field, but it will make it harder for researchers that have less financial resources to publish in top journals.

11. *Jesse Itzkowitz*:

    The field is wide open. There are very few people on the industry side that have the knowledge and abilities of academic consumer psychologists. Industry doesn't know how to access academic insights and make them actionable. The field is very nascent and there is great opportunity.

12. *Carl Marci*:

Data science, machine learning and artificial intelligence are rising. You need solid experimental and theory as a base, but the field is moving to more and more AI based tools.

13. *Steve Neumann*:

There is much talk today about artificial intelligence and leveraging "big data" through machine learning to better develop insights. For the most part, this is still talk versus reality, but there may come a day when insights can be more systematically derived from these data sets. In fact, there are those that believe that these systems will supplant consumer research people entirely in the future.

I believe this thinking is flawed. While these systems and approaches may provide good understanding of what happened, I believe that there will still be a need for consumer psychologists to understand WHY it happened, particularly in industries where there is not a followable direct transactional link between behaviors leading up to the purchase and the purchase.

The biggest challenge that consumer psychologists may encounter centers around the misconceptions of what versus why. There are so many consultants and industry thought leaders who are talking about the need to strengthen analytics and drive toward greater insights that the why and art of synthesis and interpretation get lost. Keeping a drumbeat around the importance of humans understanding humans will be the greatest challenge.

14. *Priyali Rajagopal*:
I believe that the future of consumer psychology is bright. While specific research topics that will be viewed as interesting or important will continue to evolve as consumers and their consumption practices evolve, the study of consumers will remain critically important to marketers, public policy makers and consumers themselves.

15. *Jose Ribas Fernandes*:
I can't say much since I just joined the field!

16. *Ritesh Saini*:
Difficult to see how we can bridge the gap between industry needs and how traditional CP discovery works today. Methodological diversity may help.

In future more and more discoveries are likely to come from big data revelations, and less from "a priori theorizing" driven experimental research.

17. *Neela Saldanha*:
Hopefully, it will take on new challenges such as the ones I've mentioned before—focus on the East, new geographies instead of being confined to the US.

Replicability issues—and books and learning updated to account for this.

A grand theory/framework of behavioural science will emerge.

More analytics.

18. *Gulen Sarial Abi*:

I'll answer this question in two different ways. First, I'll write how I really see the field of consumer psychology evolving in the future. Second, I'll write how I would like to see the field of consumer psychology evolving in the future.

Unfortunately, I see that it is the same scholars who publish on the same topics in the top consumer psychology journals. The field is very much dependent on few number of people and these people do not seem to be open to the people, who are not in their loop. Second, the field is still not open to the interesting research ideas on investigating consumer behavior. Although all the editors of the major consumer psychology journals indicate that there will be more room for interesting research ideas with limited process explanations, I think the reviewers are still looking for process explanations. Third, I think that there is too much witch hunting on data analyses. I do not find it right that the reviewers be aggressive, and sometimes be wrong, on criticizing research findings. I think we should regain the trust that we have for each others' research rather than trying to find statistical errors in the papers.

How I would like the field of consumer psychology evolving in the future is being it a field with many different scholars, working together, on different research questions on investigating consumer behavior. We should support the field to improve and extend. We should use different research methods. We should really support as many junior consumer psychologists as possible, not only couple of them, in order for the field to extend in the future.

I think the field has already started to change in terms of the research topics that are investigated. I believe that more research on the effect of politics, religion, and technology on consumer behavior will be conducted in the near future. The opportunities are many in terms of investigating different research topics as there will always be something to investigate about consumer behavior. However, there are also many challenges. As I mentioned before, the research we do might be considered as having an incremental contribution. It may also be challenging to enter into a group of scholars who work together in the research area that you're interested as a consumer psychologist.

19. *Julio Sevilla*:

That is a great question. With technology and specifically automation, repetitive and mechanical jobs will be replaced fast. Luckily, sophisticated, cutting edge human thinking is not easily automated so there is a space for careers such as this in the future. That being said, consumer psychologists do have the challenge to get equipped with technological tools so that we can perform higher quality, more scientifically rigorous research.

20. *Antonios Stamatogiannakis*:
    Larger samples, and a greater focus on methodology. I also believe that we may soon see broader theories that explain parsimoniously large parts of human behavior. But maybe this last part is just my hope:)

21. *Stephanie Tully*:
    I believe the field is getting more and more competitive, both for getting jobs as well as getting tenure. I expect that post docs will become more commonplace in our field. I also expect that the skills people need are growing and that even behavioral scientists who primarily do lab studies will need basic coding skills and the ability to work with secondary datasets and do more complicated analyses.

22. *Dengfeng Yan*:
    I guess it's already more technology- and data-driven and will be even more so in the future, but at the same time, I don't think technology itself will be sufficient to generate insights. So theoretical understanding and data analytics are the two engines.

23. *Meng Zhu*:
    Looks good. But I believe students who can both do hard-core math and hard-core psychology will be the type in high demand, given it's [an] era of big data and AI.

I wish to hire someone like that for our own department and hope that happens soon. I also wish to work with people like that in general and am getting there.

- maybe you can call those people good economists who truly appreciate psychology or good psychologists who also appreciate econometrics.

- these people will be hot on the market, as it's easy to tell whether they are good or bad, as the entry barrier is much higher for this group than the traditional ANOVA type consumer psychologists.

REFERENCES

Bagchi, Rajesh and Derick F. Davis (2012), "$29 for 70 items or 70 items for $29? How Presentation Order Affects Package Perceptions," *Journal of Consumer Research*, 39 (1), 62–73.

Bagchi, Rajesh and Xingbo Li (2011), "Illusionary Progress in Loyalty Programs: Magnitudes, Reward Distances, and Step-Size Ambiguity," *Journal of Consumer Research*, 37 (February), 888–901.

Hoyer, Wayne D. and Deborah J. MacInnis (2007), *Consumer Behavior*, Fourth Edition, Houghton Mifflin Company; Boston: MA.

Monga, Ashwani and Rajesh Bagchi (2012), "Years, Months, and Days versus 1, 12, and 365: The Influence of Units Versus Numbers," *Journal of Consumer Research,* 39 (1), 185–98.

Monga, Ashwani, Frank May, and Rajesh Bagchi (2017), "Eliciting Time versus Money: Time Scarcity Underlies Asymmetric Wage Rates," *Journal of Consumer Research*, 44, 4 (December), 833–52.

Monga, Ashwani and Ritesh Saini (2009), "Currency of Search: How Spending Time on Search is Not the Same as Spending Money," *Journal of Retailing*, 85, 3 (September), 245–57.

Peter, J. Paul and Jerry Olson (2017), *Consumer Behavior and Marketing Strategy*, Ninth Edition, McGraw-Hill Irwin.

Saini, Ritesh and Ashwani Monga (2008), "How I Decide Depends on What I Spend: Use of Heuristics is Greater for Time than for Money," *Journal of Consumer Research*, 34, 6 (April), 914–22.

Schiffman, Leon G. and Leslie Lazar Kanuk (2000), *Consumer Behavior*, Seventh Edition, Prentice Hall; Upper Saddle River; NJ.

INDEX

For Product Safety Concerns and Information please contact our EU
representative GPSR@taylorandfrancis.com
Taylor & Francis Verlag GmbH, Kaufingerstraße 24, 80331 München, Germany

www.ingramcontent.com/pod-product-compliance
Lightning Source LLC
Chambersburg PA
CBHW052010270326
41929CB00015B/2868